ISBN 978-0-915545-06-3
First Printing 1993
Revised Printing 2013

Published by
Stanley R. Abbott Ministries, Inc.
P.O. Box 533

To: Larry & Shelly
From: Stan Abbott

Holy Spirit Unveiled

PREFACE

*"16 For God so loved the world that He gave His only begotten Son, that whoever believes in Him should not perish, but have everlasting life." **John 3:16***

The first and greatest gift God gave to the world was His very own Son, the Word made flesh. Acceptance of this gift will deliver mankind from the power of darkness and translate them into the kingdom of Christ (***Colossians 1:13***). However, before a person can call on the name of the Lord in order to be saved, there are conditions which must be met.

*"13 For whoever shall call upon the name of the Lord shall be saved. 14 How then shall they call on Him in whom they have not believed? And how shall they believe in Him of whom they have not heard? And how shall they hear without a preacher? 15 And how shall they preach, except they be sent? As it is written: "How beautiful are the feet of them that preach the gospel of peace, Who bring glad tidings of good things!" 16 But they have not all obeyed the gospel. For Isaiah says, "Lord, who has believed our report?" 17 So then faith comes by hearing, and hearing by the word of God." **Romans 10:13-17***

In other words, in order for persons to receive or benefit from the gift of God, they must have knowledge of the gift and understand what they have learned. Without hearing about the gift, they cannot receive. Without understanding what they have heard, they cannot receive. Jesus Himself spoke on this matter,

i

*"19 When anyone hears the word of the kingdom, and
does not understand it, then the wicked one comes and
snatches away that which was sown in his heart."*
Matthew 13:19

It is when people understand what they have heard
about the kingdom that the wicked one cannot steal it from
their heart. The knowledge becomes a working, evident
part of their life. The gift truly becomes theirs.

God has given a second but equally great gift. This
gift is not for mankind in general but is a gift exclusively
for the Church. This gift is the Holy Spirit. Our lack of
knowledge and understanding of this gift has been a great
hindrance to the successful operation of the Church in the
earth. It is lack of knowledge which causes us to be
destroyed.

"My people are destroyed for lack of knowledge."
Hosea 4:6

It is not God's desire for us to be destroyed. He desires for
us to have knowledge, to understand it, and to walk in the
light of it.

The following materials are intended to present
knowledge and understanding about the Holy Spirit as a
gift from the Father. Certainly what is presented here is not
considered to be all there is to know or understand concerning this gift. This is, rather, only a small beginning to
help move us in the right direction of knowing Him as God
the Holy Spirit!

DEVELOPING RELATIONSHIPS

In developing a relationship with a person, it is important to understand who the person is and the roles in which we relate to that person. Developing a relationship entails more than knowing about a person. We have to spend time with the person, find out who the person is, and know how we are to relate to the person. Relationship development involves time and hard work, but the results are exciting and well worth it. In order to develop a relationship with God the Holy Spirit, we must understand...

...who the Holy Spirit is,

...on what basis we relate to Him,

...and how to receive from Him.

As we develop our relationship with God the Holy Spirit, He will, in turn, reveal Jesus and the Father. In this way, relationship will be developed with all three members of the God-head, God the Father, God the Son, and God the Holy Spirit.

Holy Spirit Unveiled

TABLE OF CONTENTS

Chapter Three

THE HOLY SPIRIT UNVEILED

Chapter Four

HOLY SPIRIT & THE BELIEVER

Chapter Five

MINISTRY OF THE HOLY SPIRIT

Chapter Six
RECEIVING MINISTRY FROM THE HOLY SPIRIT

Chapter Seven
MANIFESTATION OF THE SPIRIT

Chapter Eight
THE ANOINTING OF GOD

Chapter Nine
SUMMARY AND CONCLUSION

Holy Spirit Unveiled

Chapter One

KEY TO THE SUPERNATURAL

One of the most remarkable portions of scripture in the entire Bible is found in the gospel according to John. The passage is nestled in between Jesus' last supper with the disciples and His betrayal, chapters thirteen through seventeen. Supper is finished, Jesus has washed the feet of the twelve disciples, Judas has left the room after having been identified as the betrayer, and Jesus is alone with His eleven closest followers. In this setting we see a new level of intimacy between Jesus and these eleven friends as He reveals things to come.

Jesus tells them He is going away and that they know both where He is going and the way to get there. Thomas challenges Jesus by asking how they could possibly know the way. Jesus replies by explaining He is the way. Next, Jesus puzzles them by saying He is going to the Father whom they both know and have seen. Then it is Philip's turn to challenge by telling Jesus to show them the Father, and it would be enough for them. All of this conversation is spontaneous dialogue between Jesus and the eleven.

Now Jesus responds to Philip's request for Him to show them the Father with the following remarkable portion of scripture.

"9 Have I been with you so long, and yet you have not known Me, Philip? He who has seen Me has seen the Father; so how can you say, Show us the Father? 10 Do you not believe that I am in the Father, and the Father in Me? The words that I speak to you I do not speak on My own authority; but the Father who dwells in Me does the works. 11 Believe Me that I am in the Father, and the Father in Me, or else believe Me for the sake of the works themselves." **John 14:9-11**

Jesus' response to Philip's challenge unlocked the secret of a major mystery in the kingdom of God. He revealed the incredible fact that it was not His own power or ability which enabled him to minister supernaturally, *"...the Father who dwells in Me does the works..."*. It was God the Father dwelling in Him doing the works. Jesus further explained it was not just by virtue of the fact that the Father dwelt in Him, but also, He in the Father. In other words, the basis for Jesus' supernatural life and ministry was His intimate relationship with the Father.

GOD'S EXPECTATION FOR BELIEVERS

Immediately following this great revelation Jesus added,

"12 Most assuredly, I say to you, he who believes in Me, the works that I do he will do also; and greater works than these he will do, because I go to My Father. 13 And whatever you ask in My name, that I will do, that the Father may be glorified in the Son. 14 If you ask anything in My name, I will do it." **John 14:12-14**

2

Every believer is expected to bear fruit by doing the same works Christ did, *"...the works that I do he will do also...".* These are not in the believer's own power and ability, but rather Christ in the believer doing the works. A short while later in the conversation, Jesus spoke again of this expectation and how it was to be fulfilled.

> *"5 I am the vine, you are the branches: He who abides in me, and I in him, bears much fruit: for without Me you can do nothing."* **John 15:5**

Jesus clearly tells us that the ability to do the same works He did comes from His abiding in us and our abiding in Him.

In only a few verses of scripture, ***John 14:9-14***, Jesus has given us the key to the supernatural and revealed God's expectations for all believers. He showed us ***the key to the supernatural is relationship***. And He said ***every believer is expected to walk supernaturally*** just as He did. We must examine both of these revelations.

JESUS AS EXAMPLE

One of the first steps in examining both of these revelations is to research the earthly life and ministry of our example, Jesus. His life on earth was a living example of the lives we are to live. Before the Son became flesh, He shared all of the characteristics or attributes of God the Father such as omnipotence, omnipresence, omniscience, immortality, and invisibility. As we begin our research, we will soon discover some very distinguishable differences between God the Father in heaven and God the Son in His earthly form. It is our understanding of these differences which help us more fully understand the humanity of Jesus as compared with His divinity.

It is easier for most Christians to see Jesus as Emmanuel, God with us, in His earthly life and ministry rather than to see Him as Mary's son Jesus. Relating Jesus with God rather than man makes His supernatural success easily explainable: As God, He could do all things. However, this view of Christ Jesus moves us in the wrong direction for ever hoping to fulfill God's expectations for our lives as believers. We must see Jesus as man in order to follow His example as men ourselves. Let us begin by examining the entrance of the Son of God into the earth to start His life and ministry as a man.

God the Son is the second person of a Triune God. Moses spoke to the children of Israel saying,

> *"4 Hear, O Israel: The Lord our God, the Lord is one!"*
> **Deuteronomy 6:4**

The only true and living God, the God of all Christians, is this same God of Israel. This one true God is a Trinity: God the Father, God the Son, and God the Holy Spirit. He is not three gods, but one, made up of three parts.

Paul wrote,

> *"4 ...When the fullness of time had come, God sent forth His Son, born of a woman..."* **Galatians 4:4**

Jesus Himself said it this way,

> *"16 For God so loved the world, that He gave His only begotten Son, that whoever believes in Him should not perish but have everlasting life. 17 For God sent not His Son into the world to condemn the world, but that the world through Him might be saved."* **John 3:16,17**

All of Christendom accepts Jesus as this Son of God who was sent into the world. However, Jesus did not exist as flesh and blood prior to being sent into the world. Before He was sent into the earth, He existed with the Father as the Word.

> *"1 In the beginning was the Word, and the Word was with God, and the Word was God. 2 He was in the beginning with God."* **John 1:1,2**

John wrote by inspiration of the Holy Spirit twelve verses later about the Word in human form. He wrote,

> *"14 And the Word became flesh and dwelt among us, and we beheld His glory, the glory as of the only begotten of the Father, full of grace and truth. 15 John bore witness of Him and cried, saying, "This was He of whom I said, He who comes after me is preferred before me, for He was before me. 16 And of His fullness we have all received, and grace for grace. 17 For the law was given through Moses, but grace and truth came through Jesus Christ.*

*"18 No one has seen God at any time. The only begotten
Son, who is in the bosom of the Father, He has declared
Him."* **John 1:14-18**

God sent His Son into the world by sending the Word to be
made flesh, born of a virgin, as the man Jesus.

VISIBLE VERSUS INVISIBLE

The very instant the Word became flesh a distinguishable difference between Father and Son occurred. While God
the Father remained an invisible Spirit being, God the Son took
on visible fleshly form. Before we can further pursue our
research on the differences between God the Father and God
the Son, we must address a vital issue here. God the Son
became distinguishably different from God the Father. Does
that mean He stopped being God? Absolutely not! God the
Son, even though distinguishably different from God the Father, never stopped being God!

Jesus compared the Word to a seed in the New Testament. The Holy Spirit, too, inspired the same comparison in
the writings of Peter.

*"23 ...born again, not of corruptible seed but of incor-
ruptible, through the Word of God..."* **I Peter 1:23**

God the Father planted the Word as seed in the virgin Mary in
order to produce the baby Jesus. Whatever type of seed is
planted, the harvest will always be the same. If you plant corn
seed, corn will be produced; if you plant cotton seed, cotton
will be produced; and so on. God's seed, as the Word, was
planted, God was produced.

Even though Jesus was God in His earthly life and ministry, it was necessary for Him to lay aside His divine characteristics and take on human characteristics in their place.

> *"21 For since by man came death, by man also came the resurrection of the dead. 22 For as in Adam all die, even so in Christ all shall be made alive."*
>
> **I Corinthians 15:21,22**

It was the man Adam who brought sin and death into the world. Therefore, Jesus had to become a man to restore what the man Adam lost. The writer of the letter to the Hebrews amplifies this truth wonderfully. He wrote,

> *"14 Inasmuch then as the children have partaken of flesh and blood, He Himself likewise shared in the same; that through death He might destroy him who had the power of death, that is, the devil, 15 And release those who through fear of death were all their lifetime subject to bondage. 16 For indeed He does not give aid to angels, but He does give aid to the seed of Abraham. 17 Therefore, in all things He had to be made like His brethren, that He might be a merciful and faithful High Priest in things pertaining to God, to make propitiation for the sins of the people. 18 For in that He Himself has suffered, being tempted, He is able to aid those who are tempted."* **Hebrews 2:14-18**

The writer of this letter to the Hebrews explicitly tells us *"...as the children have partaken of flesh and blood, He (Jesus) Himself likewise shared in the same..."*

Setting aside His divine attributes and taking on human attributes is what makes Jesus distinguishably different from the Father. In other words, Jesus was God in the earth but chose to walk as man in order to fulfill the plan of salvation. Understanding these differences will help us relate to Jesus knowing that He was not only the Son of God but also the son of man. When we see some of the key areas in which His life was made like ours, it will cause new hope to rise in us. We will realize we really can walk like Jesus. Jesus did not remain an invisible God but became a visible man after which we can pattern ourselves.

DIE-ABLE VERSUS IMMORTAL

(NOTE: We have coined and used the word die-able instead of mortal because the word mortal means subject to death. Jesus made it clear He was not subject to death when He said,

"17 My Father loves Me, because I lay down My life that I may take it again. 18 No one takes it from Me, but I lay it down of Myself. I have power to lay it down, and I have power to take it again. This command I have received from My Father." **John 10:17,18**

He had a body that when He chose according to the will of the Father, He could give it up to die. **"Death"** could not force Him to die.)

Already we have seen divine invisibility replaced with human visibility. Next we will examine the human body which made Jesus visible.

> *"4 ...It is not possible that the blood of bulls and goats could take away sins. 5 Therefore, when He came into the world, He said, "Sacrifice and offering You did not desire, but a body You have prepared for Me... "*
>
> **Hebrews 10:4,5**

Redemption required a blood sacrifice to take away sins, and Jesus as the Word made flesh was predestined to be that sacrifice. Jesus, the Son of God, had to die for men to live. The Father made that possible by preparing a body for Him which could die. God the Father remained immortal God while Jesus set aside His immortality and took on a body which could die. Replacing immortality with die-ability is clearly another distinguishable difference between God the Father in His role as God and God the Son fulfilling His role as man.

POWERLESS VERSUS OMNI-POTENT

In addition to the two differences of invisibility versus visibility and immortality versus die-ability, we will consider omnipotence versus powerless, a difference easily seen in scripture. John recorded an incident in which Jesus was involved with the Jews. Jesus healed a paralytic at the pool of Bethesda on the Sabbath. When the Jews found out about it, they persecuted Jesus and even sought to kill Him because He had done this on the Sabbath.

> *"17 But Jesus answered them, "My Father has been working until now, and I have been working." 18 Therefore the Jews sought all the more to kill Him, because He not only broke the Sabbath, but also said that God was*

> *His Father, making Himself equal with God. 19 Then*
> *Jesus answered and said to them, "Most assuredly, I say*
> *to you, the Son can do nothing of Himself, but what He*
> *sees the Father do; for whatever He does, the Son also*
> *does in like manner. 30...I can of Myself do nothing. As*
> *I hear, I judge; and My judgment is righteous, because*
> *I do not seek My own will but the will of the Father who*
> *sent me."* **John 5:17-19,30**

Jesus told the Jews He did not have the power to do anything of Himself. In other words, in the power of His human form He did not have the ability to heal the paralytic or fulfill any other aspect of His ministry. What a shocking statement! However, it will not be shocking if we understand that Jesus was simply setting aside His Godly attribute of omnipotence as part of the plan for Him to walk as a man. He was God but chose to walk as a man in order to redeem man.

> *"21 For since by man came death, by man also came the*
> *resurrection of the dead."* I ***Corinthians 15:21***

God the Son walked in the earth as the man Jesus without power while God the Father remained omnipotent. Powerless versus omnipotent is distinguishably different.

TEMPTABLE VERSUS UNTEMPTABLE

The last difference between God the Father and God the Son we will examine is temptable versus untemptable. James wrote,

> *"13 Let no one say when he is tempted, "I am tempted of*
> *God"; for God cannot be tempted by evil, nor does He*
> *Himself tempt anyone."* **James 1:13**

One of the attributes of God is untemptability. God cannot be tempted with evil, and yet Luke told us by inspiration of the Holy Spirit that Jesus was tempted of the devil.

> *"1 Then Jesus being filled with the Holy Spirit, returned from the Jordan and was led by the Spirit into the wilderness, 2 being tempted for forty days by the devil..."*
>
> **Luke 4:1,2**

If we wrote an entire volume concerning Jesus' temptability, we would never be able to capture the simplicity and purity of the words found in the letter to the Hebrews.

> *"18 For in that He Himself (Jesus) has suffered, being tempted, He is able to aid those who are tempted."*
>
> **Hebrews 2:18**

Jesus was willing to come into this world and be made temptable, and even be tempted Himself, so He could become our faithful High Priest to help us through our temptations. In order for Him to fulfill this aspect of our redemption, He had to become distinguishably different from God the untemptable Father.

During Jesus' earthly ministry He willingly became visible, die-able, powerless, and temptable. The Father was and is and always shall be invisible, immortal, omni-potent, and untemptable. Jesus not only set aside these four divine attributes but in fact...

> *"17 ...in all things He had to be made like His brethren..."* **Hebrew 2:17**

We must re-emphasize that Jesus did not stop being God because He set aside his divine attributes and was made distinguishably different from the Father. Rather, He merely set them aside to walk in the earth as a man in order to redeem us.

Jesus was God during His earthly ministry but walked entirely as a man in all He did from beginning to end of His ministry. Whether it was casting out a legion of devils, cleansing lepers, raising the dead, speaking with profound wisdom, or overcoming sin, He was powerless to fulfill His ministry in the ability of His human form. Jesus did all that He did as a "man" by the ability of God dwelling within Him.

GOD UNITED WITH MAN

Having seen the distinguishable differences between God the Father and God the Son as Jesus in His earthly life and ministry, we can now make a summary statement about Jesus the man becoming a living example for our lives: Jesus the man was only able to fulfill His ministry because God the Father and the Spirit were one with Him! It took God uniting with man in order for man to fulfill the will of God for man. This simple, yet profound truth, is the secret to a successful Christian life. We will only be able to do the works of Christ if God is united with us: God in us and us in God. We are distinguishably different from God as men but united as one with Him to live and move and have our being. This is a relationship of unity so close that we are actually called *"one"*.

Now that we see the theological foundation for Jesus' past ministry and our present ministries being fulfilled, we need to explore the practical side. Relationship is the key to the supernatural, but it must be expressed in practical terms in order for it to be workable in our lives. Jesus walked together with the Father in a relationship of agreement, but how did the life of the Father operate in Jesus' ministry? In other words, what practically did Jesus do to get the Father's life first produced in Him and then flow through Him to others? These are questions we must answer if we are ever to translate our relationship with God into *"...the works of Christ..."*

LAW FOR LIFE TO BE PRODUCED

The answers to the above questions are found in a principle or a law designed by God for life to be produced. The law/ principle states: In order for life to be produced the Word and the Spirit must work together according to the will of God. Let us look at two illustrations of this law in the scriptures. The first illustration is found in Genesis describing creation.

> *"1 In the beginning God created the heavens and the earth. 2 The earth was without form, and void; and darkness was upon the face of the deep. And the Spirit of God was hovering over the face of the waters. 3 Then God said, "Let there be light"; and there was light."*
> **Genesis 1:1-3**

Moses told us *"...God created...",* but God is made up of three parts: Father, Word, and Spirit. We must look to other scriptures to help us amplify our understanding of the three parts' work in creation. John wrote,

> *"1 In the beginning was the Word, and the Word was with God, and the Word was God. 2 He was in the beginning with God. 3 All things were made through Him, and without Him nothing was made that was made."* **John 1:1-3**

We see the Word was with God in the beginning and was God and nothing was made without the Word. Now let us go back to the Genesis account of the beginning and fit the Word into the creation scene.

The first three verses of Genesis are a presentation of God creating *"...light..."*, natural, physical light. The first phase of this creation process was God's willingness for light to be produced. Once the will of God was clearly established, the law for life to be produced had to be put into operation.

We first see the Spirit's ministry mentioned as *"...the Spirit of God was hovering over the face of the waters..."*. Strong's Exhaustive Concordance of the Bible lists the word translated *"moved"* in the King James version of the Bible (translated *"hovering"* in the New King James) as number 7363. Strong's "Hebrew Dictionary of the Old Testament" defines the Hebrew word listed number 7363.

> 7363 **rachaph** a prim. root; to brood; by impl. to be relaxed: -- flutter, move, shake.

Similarly, the Holy Spirit was *"brooding"* over creation waiting for life to be produced. In reality we will see the Holy Spirit was waiting for the Word so that together they could produce life according to the will of the Father. Immediately following the brooding position of the Holy Spirit over creation, God released the ministry of the Word: *"...and God said, Let there be light... "*. The psalmist said,

> *"130 The entrance of Your words gives light..."*
> **Psalms 119:130**

However, this light which comes by the entrance of God's Word is spiritual. Something had to happen to the Word as spiritual light to make it natural, physical light. The simplest way to explain this "something" is to consider the nature of the Word. We have already considered the apostle Peter's writings in this matter. He wrote we are,

> *"23 ...born again, not of corruptible seed but incorruptible, through the word of God which lives and abides for ever..."* **I Peter 1:23**

Jesus Himself also spoke of the Word in these same terms of seed. He said,

> *"3 Behold, a sower went out to sow..."* **Mark 4:3**

Later in the account Jesus explained,

> *"14 The sower sows the word..."* **Mark 4:14**

Jesus is comparing the nature of the Word of God to seed in order to help us better understand how the Word works.

Almost all of Jesus' teachings compare spiritual things with natural things so we can better understand the spiritual by comparing them with what we already understand in the natural.

SEED-TIME AND HARVEST

In order for natural seed to produce a harvest of life, it must first be planted then undergo transformation from its state as seed into a root and sprout. It is this transformation process which releases the life of the harvest. Part of the law of seed-time and harvest then is: ***Seed must be planted and undergo transformation before the life of the harvest can be produced.*** This comparison between natural seed and spiritual seed will help us understand how the Word and the Spirit work together to produce life.

When God the Father spoke the Word into the dark of creation, He was actually planting "seed", expecting a harvest. The harvest He desired was natural, physical light. Whatever kind of seed you plant, the same will be the harvest. The Father planted "light" seed and, therefore, the harvest would be "light". The seed was planted as the Father spoke the Word, *"Let there be light"* or *"Light be"*, into the field of creation. Then transformation had to take place before the life of the harvest could be produced. This transformation was the Holy Spirit's ministry. He was already brooding over the dark of creation preparing the environment, waiting for the "seed". The instant the seed was planted, the Holy Spirit transformed the seed from its state as spiritual light into natural, physical light according to the will of the Father. The Word and the Spirit worked together to produce life according to the will of the Father by:

1. The Word being planted as a *"...seed..."*;

2. The Spirit transforming the seed;

3. Life being produced.

Look at the second illustration from the scripture, this time from the New Testament. It is the description of the virgin birth. Luke writes,

> *"26 Now in the sixth month the angel Gabriel was sent by God to a city of Galilee named Nazareth, 27 to a virgin betrothed to a man whose name was Joseph, of the house of David. The virgin's name was Mary..."*
> **Luke 1:26,27**

As we read the narrative, we see God's purpose in sending the angel was to put the law of seed-time and harvest into operation. The harvest God wanted produced was Jesus, the Word made flesh, and the field in which the seed was to be planted was the virgin Mary. After Gabriel explained to Mary the purpose of God, Mary asked,

> *"34 How can this be, since I do not know a man?" 35 And the angel answered and said to her, "The Holy Spirit will come upon you, and the power of the Highest will overshadow you; therefore, also, that Holy One who is to be born will be called the Son of God."* **Luke 1:34,35**

God wanted a baby to be produced. According to God's plan all aspects of the pregnancy were to be natural except for the miraculous conception. Mary was to carry the child in her womb as Elizabeth her cousin spoke by the Holy Spirit,

> "*42 Blessed are you among women, and blessed is the fruit of your womb.*" **Luke 1:42**

She was to carry the child a normal term of pregnancy and give birth to the child.

> "*4 Joseph also went up from Galilee, out of the city of Nazareth, into Judea, to the city of David, which is called Bethlehem, because he was of the house and lineage of David, 5 to be registered with Mary, his betrothed wife, who was with child. 6 So it was, that while they were there, the days were completed for her to be delivered. 7And she brought forth her firstborn Son, and wrapped Him in swaddling cloths, and laid Him in a manger.*"
> **Luke 2:4-7**

In order to have this life come into existence, God put the law for life to be produced into operation. This law produced the miraculous conception. First, the Word was planted as seed into the womb of the virgin Mary. However, words do not make babies. Something had to happen to the seed in order for the desired life to be produced. This "something" was the transformation process which we have already seen is the Spirit's responsibility. The Holy Spirit came upon Mary and transformed the seed of the Word into a living sperm cell which then joined itself to Mary's egg. After this miraculous conception, the baby Jesus began to be naturally formed.

Notice a *"practical"* difference in harvest timing between the Genesis illustration and the Virgin-Birth illustration. The harvest of light was instantaneous without any natural process of growth involved in Genesis, whereas, the harvest required natural process of growth in the Virgin-Birth. This understanding will help eliminate much frustration and doubt as we apply the law for life to be produced in our lives in the days to come. Many times after the Holy Spirit has fulfilled His ministry of transforming the seed, we must wait for processes of growth before we can reap the harvest. The transformation process may vary in time from immediate to a long period. Giving into frustration may abort the process. Patience, however, will allow the process of transformation to be completed.

> *"35 Cast not away therefore your confidence, which hath great recompence of reward. 36 For ye have need of patience, after ye have done the will of God, you might receive the promise."* **Hebrews 10:35,36**

HARVEST OF NEW BIRTH

How does this law directly apply to us? The first application is in the *"new birth"*. Paul wrote,

> *"13 For whoever calls on the name of the Lord shall be saved. 14 How then shall they call on Him in whom they have not believed? And how shall they believe in Him of whom they have not heard? And how shall they hear without a preacher? 15 And how shall they preach unless they are sent?..."* **Romans 10:13-15.**

A preacher *(any one proclaiming the good news)* must first plant seed into the hearers before they can call on the name of the Lord to be saved. The seed is planted as knowledge about Christ. This is the first half of the law in operation.

Next, the Holy Spirit must transform the seed into living relationship between the hearer and Christ. Salvation is a process beginning with a person entering into a personal relationship with Christ as Lord and Saviour. The Holy Spirit told us through Paul,

> *"3 ...no one can say that Jesus is the Lord except by the Holy Spirit..."* **I Corinthians 12:3**

Knowledge about Christ, gained through the planted seeds of the Word, will not save a person. Only living relationship with Christ will cause a person to be saved. Many Christians have tried to make the knowledge about Christ, gained through the scriptures, produce life by itself. However, without the transforming ministry of the Holy Spirit bringing a person into a relationship with Christ as the Word, life will not be produced.

Consider the seven sons of Sceva (***Acts 19:13-20***) as testimony of this simple truth. They received the seed of the Word telling them about Christ as Deliverer. They heard in Christ's name they could cast out evil spirits. With this knowledge they went to a man possessed with an evil spirit believing they could cast out the spirit. They applied their knowledge by speaking directly to the evil spirit,

> *"14 We exorcise you by Jesus whom Paul preaches."...*
> *15 and the evil spirit answered and said, "Jesus I know,*
> *and Paul I know; but who are you?" 16 Then the man in*
> *whom the evil spirit was leaped on them, overpowered*
> *them, and prevailed against them, so that they fled out of*
> *that house naked and wounded." **Acts 19:13-16***

The seven sons of Sceva only knew *"...about..."* Jesus the Deliverer. It was seed to them but had never been transformed into a living relationship with the Deliverer. The result was no life could be born through them in the area of deliverance.

In contrast, the apostle Paul spoke to a spirit of divination in a certain damsel,

> *"18 I command you in the name of Jesus Christ to come*
> *out of her. And he came out the same hour." **Acts 16:18***

What was the difference? Paul had a relationship with Christ as deliverer whereas the seven sons of Sceva only knew about Christ as deliverer. The difference between knowing about Christ and knowing Christ is the difference between life and death.

The most profound statement concerning this matter was spoken by Jesus Himself. He said to certain of the Jews,

> *"39 You search the Scriptures, for in them you think you*
> *have eternal life; and these are they which testify of Me.*
> *40 But you are not willing to come to Me that you may*
> *have life." **John 5:39,40***

Scriptures were given to us by inspiration of God and are,

> *"16 ...profitable for doctrine, for reproof, for correction, for instruction in righteousness, 17 that the man of God may be complete, thoroughly equipped for every good work."* **II Timothy 3:16,17**

We must accept the scriptures as from God but not as a substitute for God!

Scriptures are seeds telling us about God, but only the Holy Spirit can transform those seeds into relationship with God. **It is this two-step process, planting seeds of knowledge about God and the transformation of those seeds into relationship with God, that produces a harvest of life within us.**

RELATIONSHIP EQUALS LIFE

We asked the question earlier, "What did Jesus do practically to get the Father's life produced in Him"? Understanding the law for life to be produced sets the stage for us to be able to answer this question. One more piece of revelation is needed to help further our understanding. Jesus said,

> *"3 This is eternal life, that they may know You, the only true God, and Jesus Christ, whom You have sent."*
> **John 17:3**

This statement is actually an equation which will lead persons to life eternal if they understand it.

In mathematics two plus two equals four.

$$2 + 2 = 4$$

Another way of saying this is two plus two is four.

$$2 + 2 \text{ is } 4$$

In other words, whatever is on the left side of the equation is equivalent to what is on the right side of the equation. Jesus' *"equation"* says life eternal is the equivalent of knowing God and His Christ.

Life Eternal $=$ Knowing God & His Christ or

Life Eternal is Knowing God & His Christ.

Life eternal is not just living forever. Everyone will live forever either eternally separated from God or eternally with God. Life eternal is referring to quality of life more than quantity of days. In the simplest terms Jesus' equation says in order to have the quality of life like God has it, you must know God. In other words, the measure of relationship you have with God determines the measure of His life you have working in and through you. We grow in relationship with God through a two step process:

1) The planting of seeds of the Word as knowledge about God.

2) The Holy Spirit transforming those seeds into relationship with God.

Jesus grew in His relationship with the Father. Therefore, He increased the measure of the life of the Father working within Him through:

1) Seeds of knowledge about God planted in Him.

2) The transformation of those seeds into further relationship with God.

Luke wrote concerning Jesus' growth.

"41 His parents went to Jerusalem every year at the Feast of the Passover. 42 And when He was twelve years old, they went up to Jerusalem according to the custom of the feast. 43 When they had finished the days, as they returned, the Boy Jesus lingered behind in Jerusalem. And Joseph and His mother did not know it; 44 but supposing Him to have been in the company, they went a days journey, and sought Him among their relatives and acquaintance. 45 So when they did not find Him, they returned to Jerusalem, seeking Him. 46 Now so it was that after three days they found Him in the temple, sitting in the midst of the teachers, both listening to them and asking them questions. 47 And all who heard Him were astonished at His understanding and answers. 48 So when they saw Him, they were amazed; and His mother said to Him, "Son, why have You done this to us? Look, Your father and I have sought You anxiously." 49 And He said to them, "Why did you seek Me? Did you not know that I must be about My Father's business?" 50 But they did not understand the statement which He spoke to them. 51 Then He went down with them and came to

Nazareth, and was subject to them, but His mother kept all these things in her heart. 52 And Jesus increased in wisdom and stature, and in favor with God and men."
Luke 2:41-52

As difficult as it may be for us to understand, Jesus grew in His relationship with the Father through the same law of seed-time and harvest that we have seen in the *Creation*, the *Virgin-Birth*, and the *New Birth* illustrations. For us to be able to do the works of Christ, we must follow Christ as the pattern for our lives. Therefore, we must grow in knowledge and relationship with God in order to have His life produced within us.

"The people who know their God shall be strong, and carry out great exploits!"
Daniel 11:32

Chapter Two

GOD'S WILL AND FAITH

God has a will for every aspect of the life of man. He desires for man to walk supernaturally in the earth just as Jesus did. That walk begins as man enters into intimate relationship with God in order to partake of eternal life, to be born again. It is to continue on a daily basis living in the victory we obtain from our relationship with God for our own lives. It is to extend to others doing the same works Jesus did. Supernatural lives are the will of God for man. However, God's will does not work automatically in our lives!

SALVATION

The simplest illustration of this truth that God's will does not work automatically is the new birth itself. Scripture says,

> "9 The Lord is not slack concerning His promise, as some count slackness, but is longsuffering toward us, not willing that any should perish but that all should come to repentance." *II Peter 3:9*

> "16 For God so loved the world that He gave His only begotten Son, that whoever believes in Him should not perish but have everlasting life. 17 For God did not send

*His Son into the world to condemn the world, but that the world through Him might be saved. 18 He who believes in Him is not condemned; but he who does not believe is condemned already, because he has not believed in the name of the only begotten Son of God." **John 3:16-18***

It is clear that God desires for all men to be saved and that He has sent His Son Jesus to make provision for salvation. However scripture also teaches us,

*"13 Whoever calls on the name of the Lord shall be saved. 14 How then shall they call on Him in whom they have not believed? And how shall they believe in Him of whom they have not heard? 15 And how shall they hear without a preacher? And how shall they preach unless they are sent? 17...So then faith comes by hearing, and hearing by the word of God." **Romans 10:13-15,17***

Even though it is the will of God for all men to be saved, His will does not work automatically in our lives. In order for us to experience the will of God for salvation for our own lives, we must exercise faith. The will of God does not work automatically; it is activated by faith!

*"8 For by grace are ye saved through faith, and that not of yourselves; it is the gift of God." **Ephesians 2:8***

Throughout the entire Bible we see this pattern repeated. God speaks to man concerning His will for man, but that will must be activated by faith. Consider three Old Testament illustrations.

ABRAHAM

On repeated occasions God came to Abraham and revealed His will to him. He told Abraham to leave his father's house and country and go to a place He would both show and give him. He told Abraham to offer Isaac upon the altar. God revealed His will to Abraham which could have both good and bad consequences depending on how Abraham responded. However, we also know from scripture God's will for Abraham did not come to pass automatically just because God willed it. Abraham had to get involved with faith. In other words, Abraham activated what he knew to be the will of God by faith.

> *"1 What then shall we say that Abraham our father has found according to the flesh? 2 For if Abraham was justified by works, he has something to boast about, but not before God. 3 For what does the Scripture say? Abraham believed God, and it was accounted to him for righteousness."* **Romans 4:1-3**

SARAH

In similar fashion God spoke His will to Sarah regarding the miraculous conception and birth of Isaac. At first Sarah laughed because it seemed so impossible; it was even humorous. Nevertheless, God meant what He said. It was His will for Sarah to conceive and give birth to a child in her barren old age. However, His will does not work automatically. It must be activated by faith. No matter how much He wanted Abraham and Sarah to have Isaac unless they were willing to walk in faith regarding His will, His will would not come to pass in their lives.

> *"11 By faith Sarah herself also received strength to
> conceive seed, and she bore a child when she was past
> the age, because she judged Him faithful who had
> promised." **Hebrews 11:11***

WALLS OF JERICHO

God's will is not always just for an individual or a
couple. He also has a will for cities and nations. God spoke to
the Israelites regarding the promised land. He told them He
would give it to them as their inheritance. That was the
promised will of God. However, we know an entire generation
of people died in the wilderness without ever experiencing
God's will for their lives even though God had willed it. The
reason the will of God did not come to pass in their lives was
because they refused to walk in faith. **God's will does not
operate automatically in our lives: it must be activated by
faith!**

A generation of Israel finally became willing to walk in
faith concerning God's will for the promised land. Their first
test of faith was the mighty walled city of Jericho.

> *"2 And the Lord said to Joshua: See! I have given
> Jericho into your hand, its king, and the mighty men of
> valor." **Joshua 6:2***

This statement was made even while Jericho was still a mighty
walled city without so much as a stone out of place in the walls.
This was the will of the Lord for the people of Israel! However,

it. It must be activated by faith! So, the Lord gave instructions for the people to walk in their faith.

> *"3 You shall march around the city, all the men or war; you shall go all around the city once. this you shall do six days. 4 And seven priests shall bear seven trumpets of rams' horns before the ark. But the seventh day you shall march around the city seven times, and the priests shall blow the trumpets. 5 It shall come to pass, when they make a long blast with the ram's horn, and when you hear the sound of the trumpet, that all the people shall shout with a great shout; then the wall of the city will fall down flat. And the people shall go up every man straight before him."* **Joshua 6:3-5**

> *"30 By faith the walls of Jericho fell down after they were encircled for seven days."* **Hebrews 11:30**

God's desired relationship with man is clearly set down in scripture. God has a will for man, but He expects man to walk in His will by faith. His will does not operate automatically; it must be activated by faith! God wants man to have eternal life to be lived out in a daily, supernatural walk of faith.

HOW TO OBTAIN FAITH

This faith we are considering is not a natural thing but rather a spiritual thing. The Holy Spirit inspired Paul to call it *"...the gift of God...".*

> *"8 For by grace are ye saved through faith, and that not of yourselves; it is the gift of God, 9 not of works, lest anyone should boast."* **Ephesians 2:8,9**

31

All men do not have this spiritual faith as we can see from Paul's exhortation to the brethren in Thessalonica.

> *"1 Finally, brethren, pray for us, that the word of the Lord may run swiftly and be glorified, just as it is with you, 2 and that we may be delivered from unreasonable and wicked men; for not all have faith."*
>
> ***II Thessalonians 3:1,2***

God is no respecter of persons. Therefore, if all men do not have faith, it is because they have either not yet had opportunity to receive it, or they have had the opportunity and rejected it. We will consider man's first opportunity to obtain faith in New Testament times. We will see how man obtains faith in order to be saved.

FAITH & THE MINISTRY OF THE WORD

We have already seen God is willing for all men to be saved. Scripture tells us *"...whoever calls on the name of the Lord shall be saved"* ***Romans 10:13***. However, the same portion of scripture tells us,

> *"14 How then shall they call on Him in whom they have not believed? And how shall they believe in Him of whom they have not heard? And how shall they hear without a preacher."* ***Romans 10:14***

The first thing necessary, then, for a person to obtain faith in order to be saved is to find out it is Jesus the Lord Who saves them.

Once we find out Jesus is the Father's provision for salvation, there is a second thing needed for the person to obtain faith in order to be saved. The person must know what is the proper basis to relate to Jesus for salvation.

> *"12 Through one man sin entered the world, and death through sin, and thus death spread to all men, because all sinned... 17 For if by the one man's offense death reigned through the one, much more those who receive abundance of grace and of the gift of righteousness will reign in life through the One, Jesus Christ... 19 For as by one man's disobedience many were made sinners, so also by one Man's obedience many will be made righteous... 21 so that as sin reigned in death, even so grace might reign through righteousness to eternal life through Jesus Christ our Lord."* **Romans 5:12,17,19,21**
> *(See also **Philippians 2:5-11**)*

The person must learn the law of sin and death rules over everyone outside of Christ. They need to see that through Jesus' righteous obedience He has triumphed over sin and death and is now ruling as Lord of all. They must understand the proper basis to relate to Jesus for salvation is as Lord and Saviour.

Only one thing more is needed for the person to be able to obtain faith in order to be saved. They must know how to receive ministry from Jesus.

> *"9 If you will confess with your mouth the Lord Jesus and believe in your heart that God has raised Him from the dead, you will be saved. 10 For with the heart one believes unto righteousness, and with the mouth confession is made unto salvation."* **Romans 10:9,10**

The person must understand it is believing in his heart that God has raised Jesus from the dead and confessing with his mouth Jesus as Lord that causes him to be able to receive ministry from Jesus for salvation.

We know and understand it is the Father's will for mankind to be saved. We also know and understand the Father's will does not operate automatically. His will must be activated by faith. We see three things are needed for a person to obtain faith in order to be saved. A person must know and understand:

1. Who the Lord is who saves them.

2. What is the proper basis to relate to Him.

3. How to receive ministry from Him.

FAITH & THE MINISTRY OF THE SPIRIT

We have seen three things are necessary for a person to obtain faith in order to activate the will of God concerning salvation. In the same way three things are necessary for a person to obtain faith to activate the will of God concerning the Holy Spirit. A person must know and understand:

1. Who the Holy Spirit is.

2. What is the proper basis to relate to Him.

3. How to receive ministry from Him.

When the Holy Spirit was first received by the Church on the day of Pentecost, we see these three things in operation. Jesus Himself taught them to the Church just before He was taken up into Heaven.

> *"4 Being assembled together with them, He com-manded them not to depart from Jerusalem, but to wait for the Promise of the Father, "which," He said, "you have heard from Me; 5 for John truly baptized with water, but you shall be baptized with the Holy Spirit not many days from now... 8 You shall receive power when the Holy Spirit has come upon you; and you shall be witnesses to Me in Jerusalem, and in all Judea and Samaria, and to the end of the earth."* **Acts 1:4,5,8**

Jesus knew the Church needed certain knowledge and understanding in order to have faith for the ministry of the Holy Spirit to become active in their individual lives. So He taught them they were to:

1. ...wait for the Holy Spirit who is the Promise from the Father.

2. ...relate to the Holy Spirit as the one who would empower them to be witnesses of Jesus to the whole earth.

3. ...be baptized with the Holy Spirit the same way John baptized with water.

He had already explained in some detail to the disciples how the Church was to have an internal relationship with the Holy Spirit who would come to live inside each believer.

> *"16 I will pray the Father, and He will give you another Helper, that He may abide with you forever. 17 The Spirit of Truth, whom the world cannot receive, because it neither sees Him nor knows Him; but you know Him, for He dwells with you and will be in you."* ***John 14:16,17***

What Jesus taught the Church was only an introduction to the Holy Spirit. The introduction was not meant to be comprehensive of all the Church would ever need to know concerning who the Holy Spirit is, the proper basis to relate to Him, and how to receive ministry from Him. The information was simply to help the Church obtain faith for the Holy Spirit to become an active part of their individual lives. This is the same kind of introduction the individual receives concerning Jesus before they can be saved. Peter said,

> *"2 As newborn babes, desire the pure milk of the word, that you may grow thereby, 3 if indeed you have tasted that the Lord is gracious."* *I **Peter 2:2,3***

In order to be saved we must know who Jesus is, the proper basis to relate to Him, and how to receive ministry from Him. However, what we learn is only *"...a taste of the Lord..."*, an introduction, not comprehensive of all we will ever need to know concerning Jesus.

The minimal knowledge and understanding the Church needs to obtain faith for the Holy Spirit's ministry to become an active part of our lives today is the same Jesus gave the 120 believers prior to the day of Pentecost.

1. The Holy Spirit is the Promise from the Father.

2. The believers are to relate to Him as the one who will empower them to be witnesses of Jesus to the whole earth.

3. They are to be baptized with the Holy Spirit by Jesus like John baptized people with water. At the time they are immersed in the Holy Spirit, they are to receive Him to come live inside them just like they received Jesus as the Word to come live inside them at the time of their new birth.

After the believer tastes of the Holy Spirit, they are to continue to grow in knowledge and understanding of who He is, the proper basis to relate to Him and how to receive ministry from Him. Because the Holy Spirit is God the Holy Spirit and God is eternal, without beginning and without ending, our learning process will also be eternal without ending. In other words, we are never going to know all there is to know about God the Holy Spirit. However, it is the will of God for us to walk with the Holy Spirit and the Holy Spirit will reveal Himself to us according to the will of God!

Chapter Three

THE HOLY SPIRIT UNVEILED

As we begin to grow in our knowledge and understanding of the person and ministry of the Holy Spirit, there are two things we must remove that have blocked our "view" of the Holy Spirit. The first thing is regarding the concept of learning itself. All learning is by comparison. In other words, we learn new things by comparing what we desire to learn with something we already know.

The world of mathematics provides us with a perfect example. When a teacher introduces students to the idea of numbers especially adding, subtracting, multiplying, and dividing, the teacher teaches from what is known not from the abstract. In other words, the teacher will associate numbers with objects with which the students are familiar and add, subtract, multiply, or divide those objects so the students will have something with which to relate the number. The teacher may use apples. The teacher will take an apple and say this is one apple. The teacher will take another apple and say this is one apple. Then the teacher will say one apple together with another apple is two apples. The students can easily identify with apples as a part of everyday life. Now the students have something known to which they can relate the unknown world of arithmetic.

Jesus used this same principle during His earthly life and ministry. He would compare invisible spiritual things with visible earthly things to help the people understand. An excellent illustration of this is Jesus' conversation with the Pharisee Nicodemus. Jesus compares natural birth with spiritual birth. He said,

> *"3 Most assuredly, I say to you, unless one is born again, he cannot see the kingdom of God" 4 Nicodemus said to Him, "How can a man be born when he is old? Can he enter a second time into his mother's womb and be born?" 5 Jesus answered, "Most assuredly, I say to you, unless one is born of water and the Spirit, he cannot enter the kingdom of God. 6 That which is born of the flesh is flesh, and that which is born of the spirit is spirit. 7 Do not marvel that I said to you, You must be born again. 8 The wind blows where it wishes, and you hear the sound of it, but cannot tell where it comes from and where it goes. So is everyone who is born of the spirit." 9 Nicodemus answered and said to Him, "How can these things be?" 10 Jesus answered and said to him, "Are you the teacher of Israel, and do not know these things? 11 Most assuredly, I say to you We speak what We know and testify what We have seen, and you do not receive Our witness. 12 If I have told you earthly things and you do not believe, how will you believe if I tell you heavenly things?"* **John 3:3-12**

Another wonderful illustration of this principle is Jesus and His eleven disciples in the upper room after Judas left the room. Jesus is speaking very intimately with the eleven. Jesus compares the relationship of a vine and its branches to our relationship with Him. He said,

> *"1 I am the true vine, and My Father is the vinedresser. 2 Every branch in Me that does not bear fruit He takes away; and every branch that bears fruit He prunes, that*

*it may bear more fruit. 3 You are already clean because
of the word which I have spoken to you. 4 Abide in Me,
and I in you. As the branch cannot bear fruit of itself,
unless it abides in the vine, neither can you, unless you
abide in Me. 5 I am the vine, you are the branches. He
who abides in Me, and I in him, bears much fruit; for
without Me you can do nothing." **John 15:1-5**

Perhaps the most majestic illustration is what the Holy
Spirit inspired John to write on the isle of Patmos when he saw
Jesus in His glory on the Lord's day. John compares natural
items with the glorious Jesus Christ. John wrote,

*"10 I was in the spirit on the Lord's day, and I heard
behind me a loud voice, as of a trumpet, 11 saying, "I am
the Alpha and the Omega, the First and the Last," and,
"What you see, write in a book and send it to the seven
churches which are in Asia: to Ephesus, to Smyrna, to
Pergamos, to Thyatira, to Sardis, to Philadelphia, and to
Laodicea." 12 Then I turned to see the voice that spoke
with me. And having turned I saw seven golden
lampstands, 13 and in the midst of the seven lampstands
One like the Son of Man, clothed with a garment down to
the feet and girded about the chest with a golden band.
14 His head and hair were white like wool, as white as
snow, and His eyes like a flame of fire; 15 His feet were
like fine brass, as if refined in a furnace, and His voice
as the sound of many waters; 16 He had in His right hand
seven stars, out of His mouth went a sharp two-edged
sword, and His countenance was like the sun shining in
its strength." **Revelation 1:10-16**

This concept of learning by comparison is wonderful
unless the thing to be learned does not have something to which
it can easily be compared. This is the case with the Holy Spirit.
He is invisible and is not easily compared to any natural thing
or person.

41

That makes it difficult for the Church to relate to Him. This has blocked our understanding and helped to keep us from being more actively involved with the Holy Spirit.

BLOCKED BY TRADITION

The other thing which serves to block our view of the person and ministry of the Holy Spirit is a traditional understanding of the Holy Spirit. In many circles the Church learned the Holy Spirit was the power of God. Because we learn by comparison, this traditional understanding caused us to try to relate to the Holy Spirit as power in much the same way we relate to natural power.

For example, electricity is a source of power in the natural world commonplace to our every day lives. Translating this power into practical use in our lives requires some device such as a switch to be turned on so we may benefit from the power of electricity. No matter how innocently we make the comparison between electricity and the Holy Spirit the outcome is the same. We try to find the switch to turn on the Holy Spirit so we may benefit from Him as power. In a very real sense, we are trying to find ways to use the Holy Spirit like we use electricity. The Holy Spirit is not simply power to be used but is rather a person who is God and has power.

The difference between using power and relating to a person is as different as night is from day. God the Holy Spirit is not sent by God the Father to be used by the Church. The whole idea of using God is repugnant. The Israelites' lives under the old covenant are to serve as examples to us who are under the new covenant. Their lives constantly remind us how little they wanted to know their God, and how much they wanted God to do something for them. They rejoiced when God provided a miracle for them and cursed when they needed a miracle. Even though they had the presence of God with them all the time, their lives were controlled by circumstances rather than God's presence. God said of them,

> *"9 Your fathers tested Me; They tried Me, though they saw My work. 10 For forty years I was grieved with that generation, And said, It is a people who go astray in their hearts, And they do not know my ways."* **Psalms 95:9,10**

The prophet Daniel summed up their lives speaking oppositely of them when he said,

> *"32 The people who know their God shall be strong, and carry out great exploits."* **Daniel 11:32**

The generation of Israelites who died in the wilderness was not strong and did no great exploits even though they saw the awesome power of God demonstrated on the earth beyond that ever seen before by man. They knew God's acts or works but did not know Him or His ways.

Our God desires that we know Him: God the Father, God the Son, and God the Holy Spirit. We will receive blessings from our relationship with Him according to His will, but these blessings will be by-products of our relationship. Knowing God is the center of God's will. God's will is not for us to try to find out how to get Him to act a certain way on our behalf. God does want us to prosper and receive natural blessings but as by-products of our relationship with Him as God. This is a paradox just as the scripture says,

> *"33 Whoever seeks to save his life will lose it, and whoever loses his life will preserve it."* **Luke 17:33**

Jesus states this so simply and so clearly with just a few words in His prayer to the Father. He said,

> *"3 This is life eternal, that they may know You, the only true God, and Jesus Christ whom You have sent."* **John 17:3**

God wants us to benefit from the person and ministry of the Holy Spirit but not because we have found the switch and turned on the Holy Spirit. Instead, God wants us to recognize the Holy Spirit as God the Holy Spirit and desire to know Him. It is out of knowing our God, including the part of God known as God the Holy Spirit, that will make us strong and cause us to do great exploits.

Now we see the wisdom of God in telling us three things that are necessary to be able to obtain faith to activate the will of God concerning the Holy Spirit. We must know and understand:

*1. **Who the Holy Spirit is.***

*2. **The proper basis to relate to Him.***

*3. **How to receive ministry from Him.***

All of these require the Church to seek to know God the Holy Spirit and to develop relationship with the Holy Spirit as God.

WHO IS GOD THE HOLY SPIRIT

Scripture teaches us the old covenant serves as a model or type and shadow of the new covenant. That means there are things which can be more easily seen concerning the will of God if you consider the old covenant compared to the new covenant. We can make similar comparisons in the natural world. For example, plastic models of larger items.

In some nations of the world airports do not have jetways from the terminal building out to the aircraft. In such places the passengers must ride an airport bus or walk out to the airplane for departure or from the plane to the terminal upon arrival whichever the case may be. To stand on the ground beneath a 747 Jumbo Jet is an incredible experience. The plane is so enormous it is impossible to get an accurate perception of how all the parts of the plane actually fit together. However, certain companies make scaled plastic models of the huge aircraft which can be glued or snapped together and held in the hand. When holding the model in your hand, you can turn it in many different directions to see how the aircraft is actually constructed. The model helps us "see" certain perspectives of the 747 more easily than to look at the Jumbo Jet itself.

In our quest for relationship with God the Holy Spirit through knowledge and understanding provided by scripture, we will begin our search in the Old Testament as a model to help us "see" certain perspectives of the Holy Spirit more easily. The setting we will consider is the children of Israel in the wilderness. God has just delivered the Israelites from the house of bondage in Egypt. He has brought them across the Red Sea into the wilderness and has entered into covenant relationship with them. Now He is speaking to Moses regarding the building of the Temple.

> *"1 Then the Lord spoke to Moses, saying: 2 "Speak to the children of Israel, that they bring Me an offering. From everyone who gives it willingly with his heart you shall take My offering. 3 And this is the offering which you shall take from them: gold and, silver, and bronze; 4 blue, purple, and scarlet thread, fine linen, and goats' hair; 5 ram skins dyed red, badger skins, and acacia wood; 6 oil for the light, and spices for the anointing oil and for the sweet incense; 7 onyx stones, and stones to be set in the ephod and in the breastplate. 8 And let them make Me a sanctuary, that I may dwell among them.   9 According to all that I show you, that is, the pattern of the tabernacle and the pattern of all its furnishings, just so you shall make it."* **Exodus 25:1-9**

Notice the instructions of the Lord in verse nine, *"According to all that I show you, that is, the pattern of the tabernacle and the pattern of all its furnishings, just so you shall make it."*. In order for Moses to build the tabernacle he had to understand what he was commissioned to build. The Lord had to give Moses clear and specific instructions regarding the temple. Scripture says the Lord *"...showed..."* Moses and gave him a *"...pattern..."* to follow. We need to find out what the Lord showed Moses and after what the tabernacle was to be patterned.

Under divine inspiration the writer of the letter to the Hebrews in the New Testament compared the old covenant and its priesthood with the new covenant and its priesthood. At the end of this comparison the writer considers Moses and the tabernacle in the wilderness.

> *"1 Now this is the main point of the things we are saying: We have such a High Priest, who is seated at the right hand of the throne of the Majesty in the heavens, 2 a Minister of the sanctuary and of the true tabernacle which the Lord erected, and not man. 3 For every high priest is appointed to offer both gifts and sacrifices. Therefore it is necessary that this One also have something to offer. 4 For if He were on earth, He would not be a priest, since there are priests who offer the gifts according to the law; 5 who serve the copy and shadow of the heavenly things, as Moses was divinely instructed when he was about to make the tabernacle. For He said, "See that you make all things according to the pattern shown you on the mountain." But now He has obtained a more excellent ministry, inasmuch as He is also Mediator of a better covenant, which was established on better promises."* **Hebrews 8:1-6**

Verses one and two speak of the High Priest of the new covenant as a minister of the true tabernacle which the Lord built and not man. Verse one says this tabernacle is in the heavens. Then in verse four he begins a comparison between the High Priest and the true tabernacle in the heavens with the priests on earth and the tabernacle Moses built. Notice carefully he says these earthly things *"...serve the copy and shadow of the heavenly things...".* The Holy Spirit also inspires the writer to quote the Word the Lord spoke to Moses concerning *"...the pattern..."* of things God showed Moses. Here we begin to see the pattern and instructions the Lord gave Moses as being the heavenly tabernacle itself. Let us look further in the same letter to the Hebrews to see more clearly. Remember we are still comparing priesthoods in the old and new covenants.

> *"19 When Moses had spoken every precept to all the people according to the law, he took the blood of calves and goats, with water, scarlet wool, and hyssop, and sprinkled both the book itself and all the people, 20 saying, This is the blood of the covenant which God has commanded you." 21 Then likewise he sprinkled with blood both the tabernacle and all the vessels of the ministry. 22 And according to the law almost all things are purified with blood, and without shedding of blood there is no remission. 23 Therefore it was necessary that the copies of the things in the heavens should be purified with these, but the heavenly things themselves with better sacrifices than these. 24 For Christ has not entered the holy places made with hands, which are copies of the true, but into heaven itself, now to appear in the presence of God for us..."* **Hebrews 9:19-24**

Now the scripture speaks plainly concerning the pattern and instructions of the Lord to Moses. Moses saw the heavenly tabernacle itself as his pattern. The Lord instructed Moses to build a copy of the true tabernacle in heaven. With this understanding let us go back to Exodus chapter twenty-five and consider one of the vessels of ministry within the tabernacle.

> *"31 You shall also make a lampstand of pure gold; the lampstand shall be of hammered work. Its shaft, its branches, its bowls, its ornamental knobs, and flowers shall be of one piece. 32 And six branches shall come out of its sides: three branches of the lampstand out of one side, and three branches of the lampstand out of the other side. 33 Three bowls shall be make like almond blossoms on one branch, with an ornamental knob and a flower,*

*and three bowls made like almond blossoms on the other branch, with an ornamental knob and a flower and so for the six branches that come out of the lampstand. 34 On the lampstand itself four bowls shall be made like almond blossoms, each with its ornamental knob and flower. 35 And there shall be a knob under the first two branches of the same, a knob under the second two branches of the same, and a knob under the third two branches of the same, according to the six branches that extend from the lampstand. 36 Their knobs and their branches shall be of one piece; all of it shall be one hammered piece of pure gold. 37 You shall make seven lamps for it, and they shall arrange its lamps so that they give light in front of it. 38 And its wick-trimmers and their trays shall be of pure gold. 39 It shall be made of a talent of pure gold, with all these utensils. 40 And see to it that you make them according to the pattern which was shown you on the mountain." **Exodus 25:31-40**

We know by now this is a copy of something that exists in the true tabernacle in heaven. We need to find a description of the true tabernacle in order to understand after what this copy is patterned. We have such a description given to us by the Holy Spirit through John on the isle of Patmos. John was taken up to heaven into the Holy of Holies. There, in the true tabernacle which the Lord erected and not man, we see the wonders of the tabernacle through John's written description. John begins with the throne of God itself.

"2 Immediately I was in the spirit; and behold, a throne set in heaven, and One sat on the throne. 3 And He who sat there was like a jasper and a sardius stone in appearance; and there was a rainbow around the throne, in appearance like an emerald. 4 Around the throne were twenty-four thrones, and on the thrones I saw twenty-four elders sitting, clothed in white robes; and they had crowns of gold on their heads. 5 And from the throne

*proceeded lightnings, thunderings, and voices. Seven
lamps of fire were burning before the throne, which are
the seven Spirits of God."* **Revelation 4:2-5**

The copy Moses was instructed to make was *"...a
lampstand of pure gold...and six branches shall come out of its
sides: three branches of the lampstand out of one side, and
three branches of the lampstand out of the other side...You
shall make seven lamps for it...".* When John saw the real thing
after which Moses' lampstand was patterned in the true tabernacle, he was inspired to refer to it as *"...seven lamps of fire
burning before the throne...".* We know this is only a written
description of a lampstand and not really a lampstand because
immediately following these words John identifies what he
saw as *"...the seven Spirits of God...".* In other words, John
saw *"...the seven Spirits of God..."* which were manifesting
themselves so gloriously they looked like *"...seven lamps of
fire burning...".*

While John was in the true tabernacle, he beheld and
recorded many wonders. One of which we find in chapter five
also concerns the seven Spirits of God.

*"1 And I saw in the right hand of Him who sat on the
throne a scroll written inside and on the back, sealed with
seven seals. 2 Then I saw a strong angel proclaiming
with a loud voice, "Who is worthy to open the scroll and
to loose its seals?" 3 And no one in heaven or on the
earth or under the earth was able to open the scroll, or to
look at it. 4 So I wept much, because no one was found
worthy to open and read the scroll, or to look at it. 5 But
one of the elders said to me, "Do not weep, Behold, the
Lion of the tribe of Judah, the Root of David, has pre-
vailed to open the scroll and to loose its seven seals." 6
And I looked, and behold, in the midst of the throne and*

> *of the four living creatures, and in the midst of the elders stood a Lamb as though it had been slain, having seven horns and seven eyes, which are the seven Spirits of God sent out into all the earth..."* **Revelation 5:1-6**

We know the *"...Lion of the tribe of Judah, the Root of David..."* in verse five and the *"...Lamb as though it had been slain..."* in verse six to be Jesus. Verse six tells us Jesus has *"...seven horns and seven eyes, which are the seven Spirits of God sent out into all the earth...".* That means Jesus has some kind of relationship with the *"...seven Spirits of God...".* We must consider Jesus' earthly life and ministry to see if we can find anything which will help us further understand His relationship with these *"...seven Spirits of God...".*

Isaiah often wrote prophetically about Jesus and His earthly ministry and about the Spirit of God. However, many times in his writings you cannot tell whether he is prophesying about himself or about someone else. It is only as we search the scripture with the help of the Holy Spirit that we find the answer.

> *"1 The Spirit of the Lord God is upon Me, because the Lord has anointed Me to preach good tidings to the poor; He has sent Me to heal the brokenhearted, to proclaim liberty to the captives, and the opening of the prison to those who are bound; 2 To proclaim the acceptable year of the Lord, and the day of vengeance of our God; to comfort all who mourn..."* **Isaiah 61:1,2**

This continues as a lengthy Word in which we are not sure whether Isaiah is prophesying of himself or of another. We find the answer in the New Testament when Jesus reads this same portion of scripture and explains it.

> *"16 So He came to Nazareth, where He had been brought up. And as His custom was, He went into the synagogue on the Sabbath day, and stood up to read. 17 And He was handed the book of the prophet Isaiah. And when He had opened the book, He found the place where it was written: 18 "The Spirit of the Lord is upon Me, because He has anointed Me to preach the gospel to the poor; He has sent Me to heal the brokenhearted, to proclaim liberty to the captives and recovery of sight to the blind, to set at liberty those who are oppressed; 19 To proclaim the acceptable year of the Lord." 20 Then He closed the book, and gave it back to the attendant and sat down. And the eyes of all who were in the synagogue were fixed on Him. 21 And He began to say to them, "Today this scripture is fulfilled in your hearing."* **Luke 4:18-21**

Jesus was telling the people He was the one about whom Isaiah was prophesying. In other words, the Spirit of the Lord was actually upon Jesus to help Him fulfill His ministry in the earth. Here Jesus speaks of having relationship with only one Spirit of the Lord.

Let us turn again to Isaiah and see what other inspiration he had concerning Jesus and the Spirit of the Lord.

> *"1 There shall come forth a Rod from the stem of Jesse, and a Branch shall grow out of his roots. 2 The Spirit of the Lord shall rest upon Him, the Spirit of wisdom and understanding, the Spirit of counsel and might, the Spirit of knowledge and of the fear of the Lord."* **Isaiah 11:1,2**

To find out about whom Isaiah is prophesying we must trace the lineage of the Branch of which he speaks. He says the Branch who *"...shall grow out of his roots..."* is a *"...rod from the stem of Jesse...".* These are terms describing the Branch as a descendant of Jesse.

In the New Testament Paul and his party came to Antioch in Pisidia and went into the synagogue on the Sabbath. Paul ministered to the men and brethren in the synagogue concerning the descendants of Jesse.

> *"22 He raised up for them (the Israelites) David as king, to whom also He gave testimony and said, "I have found David the son of Jesse, a man after My own heart, who will do all My will." 23 From this man's seed, according to the promise, God raised up for Israel a Savior Jesus."*
> ***(See Acts 13:13-41 for entire context)***

He tells us plainly Jesus is a descendant of David. However, there is no mention of the Branch here. We know the Branch is a descendant of Jesse and David is the son of Jesse. That means the Branch and David are connected in the same lineage.

Jeremiah prophesied the Word of the Lord to the shepherds of Israel. Within the Word he wrote concerning David and the Branch,

> *"5 Behold, the days are coming," says the Lord, "That I will raise to David a Branch of righteousness; A King shall reign and prosper, And execute judgment and righteousness in the earth. 6 In His days Judah will be saved, And Israel will dwell safely; Now this is His name by which He will be called: The Lord Our Righteousness."* ***Jeremiah 23:5,6***

The prophecy clearly states the Branch is to be raised to David. The scripture tells us the Branch is to be called *"...The Lord Our Righteousness..."*. We must have one last piece of information from the New Testament to have the Branch's identity revealed. In Paul's letter to the church at Corinth he writes,

> *"30 Of Him you are in Christ Jesus, who became for us wisdom from God and righteousness and sanctification and redemption." **I Corinthians 1:30***

Now we know the Branch, the Lord Our Righteousness, is Jesus! With this revelation we will return to the prophetic Word from Isaiah and consider the Branch as Jesus in the prophecy concerning the Spirit of the Lord.

> *"1 There shall come forth a Rod from the stem of Jesse, And a Branch shall grow out of his roots..." **Isaiah 11:1***

If we replace the term ***Branch*** signifying descendant with the name ***Jesus*** the prophecy will read:

> *"1 There shall come forth a Rod from the stem of Jesse, And (**Jesus**) shall grow out of his roots. 2 The Spirit of the Lord shall rest upon Him, The Spirit of wisdom and understanding, The Spirit of counsel and might, The Spirit of knowledge and of the fear of the Lord."*
> ***Isaiah 11:2***

John wrote in ***Revelation 5:6*** when he saw Jesus in heaven that he saw Him having *"...seven horns and seven eyes, which are the seven Spirits of God sent out into all the earth..."*. If you will notice there is a striking parallel in what John saw and what Isaiah prophesied concerning Jesus in His earthly ministry. John actually saw the seven Spirits of God together with Jesus. Isaiah saw them together prophetically before Jesus was born. John said he saw *"...seven Spirits of God...".* Isaiah prophesied more specifically concerning these seven Spirits of God. He prophesied of them by name in ***Isaiah 11:2.***

The Spirit of the Lord

The Spirit of Wisdom

The Spirit of Understanding

The Spirit of Counsel

The Spirit of Might

The Spirit of Knowledge

The Spirit of the Fear of the Lord

OLD TESTAMENT MODEL

We need to understand more about these seven Spirits of God. Are they actually seven different Spirits? With the information revealed through John's and Isaiah's writings, it is impossible to discover the answer to that question. However, we can turn again to the Old Testament to serve as our model to help us find our answer.

John saw *"...Seven lamps of fire burning before the throne, which are the seven Spirits of God..."* in the true tabernacle in heaven. These seven lamps of fire burning provided the pattern for the lampstand Moses was instructed to make as the copy in the earthly tabernacle. Therefore, we can look at God's instructions to Moses concerning the model to help our understanding of the true.

"31 You shall also make a lampstand of pure gold; the lampstand shall be of hammered work. Its shaft, its branches, its bowl, its ornamental knobs, and flowers shall be of one piece. 32 And six branches shall come out of its sides: three branches of the lampstand out of one side, and three branches of the lampstand out of the other side. 33 Three bowls shall be made like almond blossoms on one branch, with an ornamental knob and a flower, and three bowls made like almond blossoms on the other branch, with an ornamental knob and a flower and so for the six branches that come out of the lampstand. 34 On the lampstand itself four bowls shall be made like almond blossoms, each with its ornamental knob and flower. 35 And there shall be a knob under the first two branches of the same, a knob under the second two branches of the same, and a knob under the third two branches of the same according to the six branches that extend from the lampstand. 36 Their knobs and their branches shall be of one piece; all of it shall be one hammered piece of pure gold. 37 You shall make seven lamps for it, and they shall arrange its lamps so that they give light in front of it. 38 And its wick-trimmers and their trays shall be of pure gold. 39 It shall be made of a talent of pure gold, with all these utensils. 40 And see to it that you make them according to the pattern which was shown you on the mountain." **Exodus 25:31-40**

The instructions to which we need to pay most careful attention are found in the following verses:

"31 ...the lampstand shall be of hammered work...shall be of one piece..."

"32 ...six branches shall come out of its sides: three branches of the lampstand out of one side, and three branches of the lampstand out of the other side..."

"36 ...all of it shall be one hammered piece of pure gold..."

"37 ...You shall make seven lamps for it..."

Moses was instructed to make one lampstand not seven lampstands. This one lampstand was to have three branches coming out of one side and three branches coming out of the other side for a total of six branches. These six branches together with the central shaft itself comprise the seven lamps. One lampstand containing seven lamps of fire burning. Seeing this "model" will help us understand the true pattern in heaven.

"FIGURE ONE"

John said he saw *"...seven lamps of fire burning..."*. According to Moses' model those seven lamps of fire burning comprised only one lampstand. The Lord God was very specific in His instructions to Moses, *"see to it that you make them (the lampstand with all its utensils) according to the pattern which was shown you on the mountain"* **Exodus 25:40**. That means what Moses received as instructions from

God and what he saw on the mountain were to be followed exactly as the pattern for the lampstand in the earthly taber-nacle. If the earthly lampstand was one lampstand containing seven lamps of fire burning, then the heavenly lampstand was one lampstand containing seven lamps of fire burning. That means what John saw in heaven was one lampstand containing seven lamps of fire burning, not seven separate lampstands.

We have already discussed the fact that John did not actually see seven lamps of fire burning but rather the seven Spirits of God. John could only use human language to de-scribe what he saw in heaven if he was going to communicate what he had seen to other men on earth. Inspired by the Holy Spirit he used the words, *"...seven lamps of fire burning..."*, to describe what he said were actually *"...seven Spirits of God..."*. Now we can use the knowledge we received from the Old Testament "model" to better understand exactly what John saw in heaven.

The earthly lampstand was only one lampstand contain-ing seven lamps of fire burning. It would be very easy to look at the earthly lampstand and say you saw seven lamps of fire burning because there are seven lamps of fire burning on the lampstand. However, it would also be accurate to say you saw one lampstand even if all seven lamps of fire were burning because all seven lamps are contained within the one lampstand.

John said he saw *"...seven lamps of fire burning..."* which are the *"...seven Spirits of God..."*. From our Old Testament model, then, we know that what John saw had to be contained within one lampstand. The seven Spirits of God are contained within one Spirit. In other words, they are not seven separate Spirits but, rather, seven manifestations of only one Spirit. John saw the one true Spirit of God! When he saw Jesus together with the "...*seven Spirits of God...*", then, he saw Jesus together with the one true Spirit of God.

Strong's Exhaustive Concordance of the Bible lists the Hebrew word Isaiah used for Lord concerning the "...*Spirit of the Lord...*" from **Isaiah 11:2** as number 3068. Strong's "Hebrew Dictionary of the Old Testament" defines the Hebrew word listed as number 3068.

> 3068 **Yehovah** from 1961; (the) self-Existent or Eternal; Jehovah, Jewish national name of God: -- Jehovah, the Lord.

The Spirit Isaiah saw prophetically in relation to Jesus was also the Spirit of the Lord God.

Let us add to our knowledge and understanding of who the Holy Spirit is by looking again at the earthly lampstand and Isaiah's prophesy. John saw "...*seven lamps of fire burning which are the seven Spirits of God...*". Not seven separate Spirits but seven manifestations of one Spirit. The instructions of God to Moses were,

> "*31 You shall also make a lampstand of pure gold; the lampstand shall be of hammered work. Its shaft, its*

branches, its bowls, its ornamental knobs, and flowers shall be of one piece."

"32 And six branches shall come out of its sides; three branches of the lampstand out of one side, and three branches of the lampstand out of the other side."

"36 Their knobs and their branches shall be of one piece; all of it shall be one hammered piece of pure gold."

"37 You shall make seven lamps for it, and they shall arrange its lamps so that they give light in front of it."

The lampstand was composed of a central shaft and three pairs of branches coming out of the sides of the shaft. The shaft of the lampstand was to have a lamp of fire and each of the six branches was to have a lamp of fire also. That made up the seven lamps for the lampstand.

Notice how carefully the Holy Spirit inspired the Word concerning this matter through Isaiah. He wrote,

"The Spirit of the Lord shall rest upon Him,

The Spirit of wisdom and understanding,

The Spirit of counsel and might,

The Spirit of knowledge and of the fear of the Lord."

The *"...Spirit of the Lord..."* is set alone at the beginning of the list. The others are grouped in three pairs. Altogether they comprise seven *"...lamps of fire burning..."*.

When we piece this information together, we see the Spirit of the Lord is the central shaft out from which the other manifestations come. The three pairs of branches coming out from the sides of the Spirit of the Lord are the Spirit of wisdom on one side paired with the Spirit of understanding on the other side; the Spirit of counsel on one side paired with the Spirit of might on the other side; the Spirit of knowledge on one side paired with the Spirit of the fear of the Lord on the other side. These six branches together with the central shaft comprise one Spirit of God: God the Holy Spirit!

What John saw in heaven was one lampstand containing seven lamps of fire burning. He saw one pure Spirit of God in seven different manifestations! Isaiah was given names for the seven manifestations of the one true Spirit of God he saw prophetically. When we ask the question, "Who is the Holy Spirit?", we can now give a scripturally based answer. The Holy Spirit is seven flames of fire burning as one Spirit of God! The Holy Spirit is,

The Spirit of the Lord

The Spirit of Wisdom

The Spirit of Understanding

The Spirit of Counsel

The Spirit of Might

The Spirit of Knowledge

The Spirit of the Fear of the Lord

Chapter Four

THE HOLY SPIRIT AND THE BELIEVER

We have just seen the Holy Spirit unveiled. What a wonderful revelation. Everything else we add to our knowledge and understanding will only increase in wonder and excitement.

THE FIRST GIFT FROM GOD

Now we want to introduce the Holy Spirit into the life of the believer. In order to do that, we must establish some things about the believer and the new covenant. The failure of the old covenant was the inability of man to walk in the covenant. This was the basis for a new covenant being given. The strength of the new covenant is God united with man so that man can walk in the new covenant in the ability of God. This union, God with man, introduces a new class of beings into the earth called "new creatures in Christ". The new creature must actually be born into the universe. This birthing process is called being born again. Peter wrote about being born again.

> *"23 Having been born again, not of corruptible seed but incorruptible, through the word of God which lives and abides forever." I Peter 1:23*

Man is born again through the ministry of the Word, not just hearing the spoken word or reading the written word, but through the ministry of the living Word. Reading or hearing about salvation alone will not cause a person to be born again. James writes about hearers only.

> *"22 Be doers of the word, and not hearers only, deceiving yourselves."* **James 1:22**

The first part of the process of being born again is hearing the Word concerning salvation.

> *"9 That if you confess with your mouth the Lord Jesus and believe in your heart that God has raised Him from the dead, you will be saved. 10 For with the heart one believes unto righteousness, and with the mouth confession is made unto salvation."* **Romans 10:9,10**

After the person has "heard" the Word, he must receive Jesus as Lord in order to be born again. The moment the person receives Jesus as Lord a miracle takes place. The power of God is released on the person's behalf and the person is born again.

> *"11 He came to His own, and His own did not receive Him. 12 "But as many as received Him, to them He gave the right to become children of God, to those who believe in His name: 13 Who were born, not of blood, nor of the will of the flesh, nor of the will of man, but of God."*
> **John 1:11-13**

It is at this time of new birth that God unites with man. Jesus comes to abide within the new believer as God the living Word. Jesus instructs His closest eleven disciples concerning His abiding presence.

"1 I am the true vine, and My Father is the vinedresser. 2 Every branch in Me that does not bear fruit He takes away; and every branch that bears fruit He prunes, that it may bear more fruit. 3 You are already clean because of the word which I have spoken to you. 4 Abide in Me, and I in you. As the branch cannot bear fruit of itself, unless it abides in the vine, neither can you, unless you abide in Me. 5 I am the vine, you are the branches. He who abides in Me, and I in him, bears much fruit; for without Me you can do nothing. 6 If anyone does not abide in Me, he is cast out as a branch and is withered; and they gather them and throw them into the fire, and they are burned. 7 If you abide in Me, and My words abide in you, you will ask what you desire, and it shall be done for you. 8 By this My Father is glorified, that you bear much fruit; so you will be My disciples."
John 15:1-8

The power of God which causes a person to be born again is the incorruptible seed, the Word of God, as Peter has already told us in ***I Peter 1:23***. The Word coming to abide within the believer is God uniting with man.

"1 In the beginning was the Word, and the Word was with God, and the Word was God." ***John 1:1***

A person is born again when the Word who is God comes to dwell within him. It is His abiding presence, together with the faith He gives us, which causes us to be able to walk in the new covenant. Paul wrote by inspiration of the Holy Spirit to the church at Corinth concerning the mystery of this wisdom of God.

"7 We speak the wisdom of God in a mystery, the hidden wisdom which God ordained before the ages for our glory, 8 which none of the rulers of this age knew; for had they known, they would not have crucified the Lord of glory." ***I Corinthians 2:7,8***

65

The rulers of this age would not have crucified the Lord of glory if they had understood the wisdom of God concerning our salvation. It is through Jesus' death that we are born again as the presence of God the living Word comes to dwell within us: God uniting with man. It is by His abiding presence that we can live in the new covenant, redeemed from the power of darkness.

> *"13 He has delivered us from the power of darkness and conveyed us into the kingdom of the Son of His love, 14 in whom we have redemption through His blood, the forgiveness of sins."* **Colossians 1:13,14**

If the Church gains understanding of this revelation it will open the door for us to walk in the earth just like Jesus.

Our salvation is a result of receiving the first gift God has given to mankind, Jesus the Word made flesh. It is this separation from the world which makes us ready to receive the second gift God has given to the Church, the Holy Spirit. We have spent a great deal of time coming to the understanding that God's will for man does not operate automatically; it must be activated by faith. Man does not receive God's first gift automatically, nor does man receive God's second gift automatically. Both gifts must be received by faith through knowledge and understanding of the gifts.

Jesus spoke to His disciples concerning the second gift, the Holy Spirit.

> *"15 If you love Me, keep My commandments. 16 And I will pray the Father, and He will give you another*

> *water said to me, "Upon whom you see the Spirit de-*
> *scending, and remaining on Him, this is Helper, that He*
> *may abide with you forever 17 the Spirit of truth, whom*
> *the world cannot receive, because it neither sees Him nor*
> *knows Him; but you know Him, for He dwells with you*
> *and will be in you. ...26 But the Helper, the Holy Spirit,*
> *whom the Father will send in My name..."*
> **John 14:15-17,26**

Notice how Jesus makes it clear the Holy Spirit is not a gift for the world. The world cannot receive Him. The Holy Spirit is a gift exclusively for the Church. Luke records Jesus speaking in another context of the Holy Spirit as a gift from the heavenly Father to His children.

> *"9 I say to you, ask, and it will be given to you; seek, and*
> *you will find; knock, and it will be opened to you. 10 For*
> *everyone who asks receives, and he who seeks finds, and*
> *to him who knocks it will be opened. 11 If a son asks for*
> *bread from any father among you, will he give him a*
> *stone? or if he asks for a fish, will he give him a serpent*
> *instead of a fish? 12 Or if he asks for an egg, will he offer*
> *him a scorpion? 13 If you then, being evil, know how to*
> *give good gifts to your children, how much more will your*
> *heavenly Father give the Holy Spirit to those who ask*
> *Him!" **Luke 11:9-13***

There are certain aspects of the Holy Spirit's ministry which operate on behalf of the believer because the person receives the Word. An example of this would be the new birth. The Holy Spirit is involved in our new birth much the same way He was involved in the conception of Jesus in the womb of the virgin Mary. The Holy Spirit became involved in the conception because Mary received the Word into her life. When a person is born again, he is not receiving the Holy Spirit into his life but is rather receiving Jesus as the Word into his life. The

Holy Spirit becomes involved in the new birth because the person receives the Word. However, for the Holy Spirit to come dwell in the believer as a gift from the Father He must be received by faith just like the believer receives the Word to come dwell in him by faith.

THE SECOND GIFT FROM GOD

Now let us introduce the Holy Spirit into the life of the believer as a gift from the Father. In Chapter Two we considered Jesus' instructions to the believers just before He was taken up into heaven. We will reconsider these instructions in the light of what we have learned about the Holy Spirit.

> *"4 And being assembled together with them, He commanded them not to depart from Jerusalem, but to wait for the Promise of the Father, "which" He said, "you have heard from Me; 5 for John truly baptized with water, but you shall be baptized with the Holy Spirit not many days from now."* **Acts 1:4,5**

Jesus told the believers not to leave Jerusalem until they had received the promise of the Father. He told them the promise would come not many days from then, at which time they were to be baptized with the Holy Spirit. John recorded John the Baptist as saying Jesus would baptize the believers with the Holy Spirit.

> *"29 Behold! The Lamb of God who takes away the sin of the world! 30 This is He of whom I said, After me comes a Man who is preferred before me, for He was before me. 31 I did not know Him; but that He should be revealed to Israel, therefore I came baptizing with water." 32 And John bore witness, saying, "I saw the Spirit descending from heaven like a dove, and He remained*

*upon Him. 33 I did not know Him, but He who sent me to baptize with He who baptizes with the Holy Spirit." 34 "And I have seen and testified that this is the Son of God." **John 1:29-34***

These verses alone do not give us enough information to give clear understanding as to all that was going to happen at the time of this Holy Spirit baptismal. We must look again at the instructions Jesus gave His eleven closest disciples at the last supper. He told them,

"15 If you love Me, keep My commandments. 16 And I will pray the Father, and He will give you another Helper, that He may abide with you forever 17 the Spirit of truth, whom the world cannot receive, because it neither sees Him nor knows Him; but you know Him, for He dwells with you and will be in you. ...26 The Helper, the Holy Spirit, whom the Father will send in My name..."
John 14:15-17,26

Let us piece all this information together. On the day of Pentecost the believers were to receive the promise of the Father, the Holy Spirit. This is how they would receive. Firstly, they were waiting with the purpose of receiving the Holy Spirit as a gift from the Father. Jesus would baptize each of them, immersing them in or covering them with the Holy Spirit. This immersion or covering is external. Since the Holy Spirit was to be in them, at the time of their baptism, they had to receive the Holy Spirit by faith to come dwell in them. The Holy Spirit as a gift from the Father comes to dwell in the believer when the believer receives the Holy Spirit by faith to come dwell in him.

It is vitally important to understand the gift from the Father is the Holy Spirit. Each believer who receives the gift receives the indwelling presence of God the Holy Spirit. Now that we know who the Holy Spirit is we can express that another way. We can say the Holy Spirit dwells in the believer as seven flames of fire burning! He dwells in the believers as:

The Spirit of the Lord

The Spirit of Wisdom

The Spirit of Understanding

The Spirit of Counsel

The Spirit of Might

The Spirit of Knowledge

The Spirit of the Fear of the Lord

Let us take a closer look at the One who dwells within us as seven flames of fire burning. Let us examine each flame of fire as it relates to us as believers. In order to make such an examination we must consider the way language has been used to speak of these seven manifestations of the Spirit. Languages generally all have a way of forming a possessive construction, words put together to identify ownership or source from which a thing or person comes. In English one way to form such a construction is with the word '...*of...*'. For example, "...*a piece of pie...*".

In this example the 'piece' is the possession of the pie or the pie is the source from which the 'piece' comes. Another example would be, "...*the President of the United States of America....*". In this example the 'President' is the possession of the United States of America or the United States of America is the source from which the 'President' comes. This type of construction serves to identify more clearly the thing or person possessed. Whose President is he? He is the United States of America's President.

The Old Testament was written in the Hebrew language. The New Testament was written in the Greek language. When scripture was translated from Hebrew and Greek to English, the translators were required to be faithful in translation. That means they had to convey the intended meaning of the writer as accurately as their skill and inspiration allowed.

We have considered many scriptures from both the Old and New Testaments regarding the Holy Spirit.

"...the Spirit of God..." **Genesis 1:2**

"...the Spirit of Truth..." **John 14:17**

"...the seven Spirits of God..." **Revelation 4:5**

"...the Spirit of the Lord God..." **Isaiah 61:1**

"...the Spirit of the Lord..." **Luke 4:18**

"...the Spirit of the Lord..." **Isaiah 11:2**

"...the Spirit of wisdom and understanding..." **Isaiah 11:2**

"...the Spirit of counsel and might..." **Isaiah 11:2**

"...the Spirit of knowledge and of the fear of the Lord..."
Isaiah 11:2

The translators have conveyed the meaning of the writers from Hebrew and Greek to English in each of these scriptures using the possessive construction formed by using the word "...of...". Now we can examine each use of this construction to help further understand the Holy Spirit as He relates to us as believers.

As we begin our examination of the seven flames of the Holy Spirit, we must insert a reminder here. Our God is a triune being, three separable, identifiable and co-equal parts, yet one God. In Chapter One we considered distinguishable differences between God the Father and God the Word made flesh. It was easy to see their distinguishing characteristics. Even though different, they are still two of the three parts of One God. Now we want to consider the third part of the Trinity, God the Holy Spirit. As we examine His defining characteristics, we will always keep in mind He is one of the three co-equal parts of our Triune God.

THE SPIRIT OF THE LORD

We will consider first the Spirit of the Lord. According to the way the writer was inspired to put these words together we know this is a possessive construction. Because of that we know certain things about the words that were put together. We know the Spirit is the Lord's or the Lord is the source from which the Spirit comes. Remember the Spirit of the Lord is a co-equal member of the Triune God. In using the possessive construction, Spirit of the Lord, God our Father is revealing something about God the Holy Spirit which will help us in our relationship with all three parts of the Trinity.

Jesus presents a clear and concise understanding of this matter in only a few words as He speaks intimately to the eleven apostles of the Lamb. He begins in John chapter fourteen verse fifteen to speak of a Helper who will come from the Father at the request of Jesus. In the remainder of chapter fourteen and continuing on into chapters fifteen and sixteen Jesus reveals the identity of the Helper as the Spirit of Truth who is the Holy Spirit. Then He said,

> *"13 When He, the Spirit of truth, has come, He will guide you into all truth; for He will not speak on His own authority, but whatever He hears He will speak; and He will tell you things to come. 14 He will glorify Me, for He will take of Mine and declare it to you. 15 All things that the Father has are Mine. Therefore I said that He will take of Mine and declare it to you."* ***John 16:13-15***

The Holy Spirit is referred to as the Spirit of the Lord to reveal to us how He will not *"...speak of His own authority, but whatever He hears He will speak; and He will tell you things to come. He will glorify Me (Jesus), for He will take of Mine and declare it to you..."*. The Holy Spirit as the Spirit of the Lord or the Lord's Spirit is to minister to us as believers on behalf of the Lord not on His own behalf.

We see the first manifestation of this demonstrated on the day of Pentecost. The believers were assembled together awaiting the promise of the Father as per Jesus' instructions. Suddenly, scripture says, like a rushing mighty wind the Holy Spirit entered the room.

> *"4 And they were all filled with the Holy Spirit and began to speak with other tongues, as the Spirit gave them utterance. 5 And there were dwelling in Jerusalem Jews, devout men, from every nation under heaven. 6 And when this sound occurred, the multitude came together, and were confused, because everyone heard them speak in his own language. 7 Then they were all amazed and marveled, saying to one another, "Look, are not all these who speak Galileans? 8 And how is it that we hear, each in our own language in which we were born? 9 Parthians and Medes and Elamites, those dwelling in Mesopotamia, Judea and Cappadocia, Pontus and Asia, 10 Phrygia and Pamphylia, Egypt and the parts of Libya adjoining Cyrene, visitors from Rome, both Jews and proselytes, 11 Cretans and Arabs, we hear them speaking in our own tongues the wonderful works of God."* **Acts 2:4-11**

The Holy Spirit gave the believers utterance speaking *"...the wonderful works of God..."*. The Holy Spirit as the Spirit of the Lord was glorifying the Lord! The Holy Spirit will always minister in the Church age as the Lord's Spirit on behalf of the Lord, not on His own authority!

THE SPIRIT OF WISDOM

Now we will consider the Spirit of Wisdom. Again, with the possessive construction we know the Spirit is Wisdom's or Wisdom is the source from which the Spirit comes. This construction is a revelation of something about God the Holy Spirit which will help us as believers.

Wisdom is defined as insight into the true nature of things. Created beings grow in wisdom. It is even said of Jesus living as a man on the earth,

*"52 And Jesus increased in wisdom and stature, and in favor with God and men." **Luke 2:52***

However, God does not increase or grow in wisdom. He is without beginning or ending. He is wisdom. This type of understanding is seen in scripture in other places. God is love. God is light. God is truth.

As wisdom God is the source of all wisdom. The Holy Spirit as the Spirit of Wisdom does not just have wisdom but is the very Spirit of Wisdom. Look at what scripture says about wisdom.

"13 Happy is the man who finds wisdom..."
Proverbs 3:13

"19 The Lord by wisdom founded the earth..."
Proverbs 3:19

*"7 Wisdom is the principle thing; Therefore get wisdom" **Proverbs 4:7***

"11 For wisdom is better than rubies, And all the things one may desire cannot be compared with her."
Proverbs 8:11

"16 How much better to get wisdom than gold!"
Proverbs 16:16

*"3 Through wisdom a house is built..." **Proverbs 24:3***

The Father has sent the Spirit of Wisdom as a gift to the Church. Think of it, the very Spirit of Wisdom is dwelling within you right now. The same Spirit who inspired Solomon with wisdom dwells in you as the Spirit of Wisdom to inspire you with the wisdom of God.

THE SPIRIT OF UNDERSTANDING

Now to consider the Spirit of Understanding. The same possessive construction used here causes us to know the Spirit is Understanding's or Understanding is the Source from which the Spirit comes. Understanding is defined as the quality of comprehension. The same fundamental we learned for wisdom applies to understanding. God did not grow or increase in understanding, He is understanding. As we consider the Spirit of Understanding, there is an important aspect of this Spirit to observe. It is paired with the Spirit of Wisdom.

Remember what Isaiah prophesied concerning Jesus and His earthly ministry.

> "2 The Spirit of the Lord shall rest upon Him, The Spirit of Wisdom and understanding..." **Isaiah 11:2**

Wisdom and understanding go together as one pair of branches. Look at what scripture says about them.

> "13 Happy is the man who finds wisdom, And the man who gains understanding." **Proverbs 3:13**

> "19 The Lord by wisdom founded the earth; By understanding He established the heavens." **Proverbs 13:19**

> "5 Get wisdom! Get understanding! Do not forget, nor turn away from the words of my mouth. 6 Do not forsake her, and she will preserve you; Love her, and she will keep you. 7 Wisdom is the principle thing; Therefore get wisdom. And in all your getting, get understanding." **Proverbs 4:5-7**

"4 Say to wisdom, "You are my sister," And call under-standing your nearest kin." **Proverbs 7:4**

"1 Does not wisdom cry out, And understanding lift up her voice?" **Proverbs 8:1**

"23 To do evil is like sport to a fool, But a man of understanding has wisdom." **Proverbs 10:23**

"16 How much better to get wisdom than gold! And to get understanding is to be chosen rather than silver." **Proverbs 16:16**

"3 Through wisdom a house is built, And by understand-ing it is established." **Proverbs 24:3**

Two branches function together, the Spirit of Wisdom and the Spirit of Understanding. God the Holy Spirit works in the believer to not only be the source of wisdom but also the understanding of that wisdom. That gives the believer the opportunity to lack neither wisdom nor understanding.

THE SPIRIT OF COUNSEL

Now consider the Spirit of Counsel. The possessive construction tells us the Spirit is Counsel's or Counsel is the source from which the Spirit comes. Counsel is defined as advice or guidance.

"11 The counsel of the Lord stands forever, The plans of His heart to all generations." **Psalms 33:11**

"24 You will guide me with Your counsel." **Psalms 73:24**

"14 Where there is no counsel, the people fall; But in the multitude of counselors there is safety." **Proverbs 11:14**

"15 The way of a fool is right in his own eyes, But he who heeds counsel is wise." **Proverbs 12:15**

"22 Without counsel, plans go awry, But in the multitude of counselors they are established." **Proverbs 15:22**

"20 Listen to counsel and receive instruction, That you may be wise in your latter days." **Proverbs 19:20**

"21 There are many plans in a man's heart, nevertheless the Lord's counsel that will stand." **Proverbs 19:21**

God the Holy Spirit dwells in the believer to give counsel. He is a ready source of advice and guidance that He receives from Jesus and the Father.

THE SPIRIT OF MIGHT

Now consider the Spirit of Might. The possessive construction tells us the Spirit is Might's or Might is the source from which the Spirit comes. Might is defined as force, power, or strength. The Spirit of Might is paired with the Spirit of Counsel as Isaiah prophesied,

"2 The Spirit of the Lord shall rest upon Him, The Spirit of Wisdom and Understanding, The Spirit of Counsel and Might." 18 "Plans are established by counsel; By wise counsel wage war." **Proverbs 20:18**

"6 For by wise counsel you will wage your own war, And in a multitude of counselors there is safety."
                                                    Proverbs 24:6

78

"18 Plans are established by counsel; By wise counsel wage war." **Proverbs 20:18**

"6 For by wise counsel you will wage your own war, And in a multitude of counselors there is safety."
Proverbs 24:6

Paired and functioning together, counsel and might dwell in the believer. Not only is the Holy Spirit the believer's source of advice and guidance, but He also gives the power and strength for the believer to be able to walk in the counsel He gives.

THE SPIRIT OF KNOWLEDGE

Now consider the Spirit of Knowledge. The possessive construction tells us the Spirit is Knowledge's or Knowledge is the source from which the Spirit comes. The Triune God we love and serve is omniscient, all knowing.

"5 Great is our Lord, and mighty in power; His understanding is infinite." **Psalms 147:5**

"28 Have you not known? Have you not heard? The everlasting God, the Lord, The Creator of the ends of the earth, Neither faints nor is weary. His understanding is unsearchable." **Isaiah 40:28**

"12 Who has measured the waters in the hollow of His hand, Measured heaven with a span And calculated the dust of the earth in a measure? Weighed the mountains in scales And the hills in a balance? 13 Who has directed the Spirit of the Lord, Or as His counselor has taught Him? 14 With whom did He take counsel, and who instructed Him, and taught Him in the path of justice? Who taught Him knowledge, And showed Him the way of understanding?" **Isaiah 40:12-14**

No one taught the Lord God. He is without beginning or ending. He does not just have knowledge; He is knowledge. God the Holy Spirit shares in this omniscience. As the Spirit of Knowledge He draws from this omniscience in order to instruct us as believers.

The knowledge of the Spirit of Knowledge includes understanding of the Trinity. He gives us this knowledge that we may know our God and have eternal life.

> *"9 Eye has not seen, nor ear heard, Nor have entered into the heart of man the things which God has prepared for those who love Him. 10 But God has revealed them to us through His Spirit. For the Spirit searches all things, yes, the deep things of God."*
>
> ***I Corinthians 2:9,10***

> *"3 This is eternal life, that they may know You, the only true God, and Jesus Christ whom You have sent."*
>
> ***John 17:3***

What an awe inspiring thought that the Spirit of Knowledge abides within us and is commissioned to instruct us with His knowledge.

THE SPIRIT OF THE FEAR OF THE LORD

Now consider the Spirit of the Fear of the Lord. The possessive construction tells us the Spirit is the Fear of the Lord's or the Fear of the Lord is the source from which the Spirit comes. The Spirit of the Fear of the Lord is paired with the Spirit of Knowledge as Isaiah prophesied,

"2 The Spirit of the Lord shall rest upon Him, the Spirit of Wisdom and Understanding, the Spirit of Counsel and Might, the Spirit of Knowledge and of the Fear of the Lord." **Isaiah 11:2**

These two branches work together in a very wonderful way. In order to discover just how they work together, we can look in scripture for the answer.

7 "The fear of the Lord is the beginning of knowledge, But fools despise wisdom and instruction." **Proverbs 1:7**

10 "The fear of the Lord is the beginning of wisdom." **Psalms 111:10**

10 "The fear of the Lord is the beginning of wisdom, And the knowledge of the Holy One is understanding." **Proverbs 9:10**

33 "The fear of the Lord is the instruction of wisdom, And before honor is humility." **Proverbs 15:33**

Without the Fear of the Lord knowledge will only puff up those receiving instruction. However, if we will yield to the Spirit of the Fear of the Lord, He will work the fear of the Lord in us and then instruct us in the knowledge of God.

The Fear of the Lord is such a powerful revelation. The Holy Spirit has inspired much to be said and written concerning it.

9 "The fear of the Lord is clean, enduring forever." **Psalms 19:9**

13 "He will bless those who fear the Lord, Both small and great." **Psalms 115:13**

"19 He will fulfill the desire of those who fear Him: He also will hear their cry and save them." **Psalms 145:19**

"11 The Lord takes pleasure in those who fear Him, In those who hope in His mercy." **Psalms 147:11**

"13 The fear of the Lord is to hate evil; Pride and arrogance and the evil way And the perverse mouth I hate." **Proverbs 8:13**

"27 The fear of the Lord prolongs days, But the years of the wicked will be shortened." **Proverbs 10:27**

"26 In the fear of the Lord there is strong confidence, And His children will have a place of refuge. 27 The fear of the Lord is a fountain of life, To turn one away from the snares of death." **Psalms 14:26,27**

"16 Better is a little with the fear of the Lord, Than great treasure with trouble." **Proverbs 15:16**

"6 In mercy and truth Atonement is provided for iniquity; And by the fear of the Lord one departs from evil."
Proverbs 16:6

"23 The fear of the Lord leads to life, And he who has it will abide in satisfaction; He will not be visited with evil." **Proverbs 19:23**

"4 By humility and the fear of the Lord Are riches and honor and life." **Proverbs 22:4**

We can see the fear of the Lord is involved in a great many aspects of life. Knowing that adds to the blessing of having the Spirit of the Fear of the Lord abiding within us. He is eager to bring the fear of the Lord into manifestation into our lives as we learn how to yield to Him dwelling within us.

MYSTERY OF GOD UNITED WITH MAN

A natural thinking person will see how difficult it is to understand how God can unite with man by coming to live within us. In fact, scripture speaks a remarkable thing about the natural part of man.

> *"9 Eye has not seen, nor ear heard, nor have entered into the heart of man the things which God has prepared for those who love Him. 10 But God has revealed them to us through His Spirit... 14 "The natural man does not receive the things of the Spirit of God, for they are foolishness to him; nor can he know them, because they are spiritually discerned."* **I Corinthians 2:9,10,14**

For the natural man the mysteries of God are too great to be understood. Even Solomon could not comprehend the mystery of God's indwelling presence in the temple built on earth. In Solomon's prayer of dedication upon completion of the temple in Jerusalem He prayed:

> *"17 And now, O Lord God of Israel, let Your word come true, which You have spoken to Your servant David. 18 But will God indeed dwell with men on the earth? Behold, heaven and the heaven of heavens cannot contain You. How much less this temple which I have built!"*
> **II Chronicles 6:17,18**

Without the ministry of the Holy Spirit to reveal this great mystery to us, we will only mentally assent to the indwelling presence of God the Word and God the Holy Spirit. Mentally assenting to God's indwelling presence will never produce the results of knowing God in order to be strong and do exploits. It is only as the Holy Spirit divinely reveals the truth of this mystery that we will come to know God who abides within us and in heaven. Our heavenly Father has willed for God the Holy Spirit to reveal these things to all who seek with a pure heart!

Chapter Five

MINISTRY OF
THE HOLY SPIRIT

We are on a quest for knowledge and understanding concerning the person and ministry of the Holy Spirit. We are searching for three things in order to obtain faith to activate the will of God concerning the Spirit in our lives. We are searching for revelation regarding:

1. Who the Holy Spirit is.

2. What is the proper basis to relate to Him.

3. How to receive ministry from Him.

Chapter Four has given us a scriptural foundation for understanding who the Holy Spirit is. Now we want to see what is the proper basis to relate to Him. The simplest, most profound statement we can make in the matter is this: ***The only basis to relate to the Holy Spirit is according to the will of God!***

GOD'S WILL & JESUS

During Jesus' earthly walk and ministry, He never stopped telling man He had come to do the will of the Father who had sent Him. Whether it was preaching in the synagogues, healing the sick, or praying in Gethsemane, everything Jesus did was what the Father willed. Let us look at scripture regarding the submission of Jesus to the Father's will in many areas of His life.

Jesus Coming to Earth:

*"38 For I have come down from heaven, **not to do My own will, but the will of Him who sent me**. 39 This is the will of the Father who sent Me, that of all He has given Me I should lose nothing, but should raise it up at the last day. 40 And this is the will of Him who sent Me, that everyone who sees the Son and believes in Him may have everlasting life; and I will raise him up at the last day."*
John 6:38-40

Jesus' Works of Ministry:

*"19 Jesus answered and said to them, "Most assuredly, I say to you, **the Son can do nothing of Himself, but what He sees the Father do; for whatever He does, the Son also does in like manner**. 20 For the Father loves the Son, and shows Him all things that He Himself does; and He will show Him greater works than these, that you may marvel. 21 **For as the Father raises the dead and gives life to them, even so the Son gives life to whom He will.** 22 For the Father judges no one, but has committed all judgment to the Son, 23 that all should honor the Son just as they honor the Father. He who does not honor the Son does not honor the Father who sent Him. ...30 **I can of Myself do nothing. As I hear, I judge**; and My judgment is righteous, because **I do not seek My own will but the will of the Father who sent Me."** John 5:19-23,30*

Jesus Praying for His Disciples:

*"6 I have manifested Your name to the men whom You have given Me out of the world. **They were Yours, You***

gave them to Me, and they have kept Your word. 7 Now they know that all things which You have given Me are from You. 8 For I have given to them the words which You have given Me; and they have received them, and have known surely that I came forth from You; and they have believed that You sent Me." John 17:6-8

Jesus as Lord and Christ:

"36 Therefore let all the house of Israel know assuredly that God has made this Jesus, whom you crucified, both Lord and Christ. 37 Now when they heard this, they were cut to the heart, and said to Peter and the rest of the apostles, "Men and brethren what shall we do?" 38 Then Peter said to them, "Repent, and let every one of you be baptized in the name of Jesus Christ for the remission of sins." Acts 2:36-38

Every area of Jesus' life was a reflection of the Father's will. That means Jesus could only do what the Father willed and man could only relate to Jesus according to the Father's will. For example, a man and his son came to Jesus for Jesus to cast a devil out of the son. Jesus cast the devil out. This could only have taken place because it was the Father's will for Jesus to cast out devils on the earth. Another example would be salvation. God the Father made Jesus Lord. That is the only reason you and I can call on Jesus as Lord in order to be saved.

GOD'S WILL & THE HOLY SPIRIT

In exactly the same way Jesus was sent by the Father to do the Father's will, so too, the Holy Spirit is sent by the Father to do the Father's will. We must discover what the Father has willed for the Holy Spirit in relation to us as believers. That will determine the proper basis for us to relate to the Holy Spirit.

There are many scriptures, both Old and New Testaments, which speak of the Holy Spirit's ministry in the earth. Perhaps the most concentrated and concise statements regarding the Holy Spirit for our search, are Jesus' words to His closest eleven disciples at His last supper with them. We will use John chapters fourteen through sixteen as our primary references. The words concerning the Holy Spirit begin in *John 14:15*.

> *"15 If you love Me, keep My commandments. 16 And I will pray the Father, and He will give you another Helper, that He may abide with you forever, 17 the Spirit of truth, whom the world cannot receive, because it neither sees Him nor knows Him; but you know Him, for He dwells with you and will be in you. ...26 But the Helper, the Holy Spirit, whom the Father will send in My name..."* **John 14:15-17,26**

The first thing we must consider here is found in verse sixteen. The Father is sending the Holy Spirit as an answer to Jesus' prayer. Jesus prayed because He knew the Church would need the Holy Spirit in order to walk in the New Covenant.

While Jesus walked on earth with the disciples, He kept them in the Father's name. However, He knew He was going away from the disciples not to walk with them on earth in the same way any longer.

> *"33 Little children, I shall be with you a little while longer. You will seek Me; and as I said to the Jews,*

> *"Where I am going, you cannot come," so now I say to you."* **John 13:33**

> *"11 Now I am no longer in the world, but these are in the world, and I come to You. Holy Father, keep through Your name those whom You have given Me, that they may be one as We are. 12 While I was with them in the world, I kept them in Your name. Those whom You gave Me I have kept; and none of them is lost except the son of perdition, that the Scripture might be fulfilled. 13 But now I come to You, and these things I speak in the world, that they may have My joy fulfilled in themselves."* **John 17:11-13**

Jesus knew the disciples must have someone to walk with them similar to the way He had in His earthly ministry. That someone was the Holy Spirit. Jesus interceded on behalf of the Church and the Father responded. ***The Father sent the Holy Spirit as a gift to the Church because Jesus interceded on our behalf!***

TRIUNE GOD

At many points in this book we are going to rehearse a fundamental truth about our God. Our God is a Triune God made up of three identifiable and separable parts, yet one God. He is Father, Word, and Spirit. Our own lives give testimony of this truth having been created in the image of the one true God. We are tripartite beings made up of three separable and identifiable parts, yet one being. We are spirit, soul, and body. Scripture speaks of these parts, identifiable and separable.

> *"12 For the word of God is living and powerful, and sharper than any two-edged sword, piercing even to the division of soul and spirit, and of joints and marrow, and is a discerner of the thoughts and intents of the heart."*
> **Hebrews 4:12**

"2 I know a man in Christ who fourteen years ago whether in the body I do not know, or whether out of the body I do not know, God knows such a one was caught up to the third heaven." **II Corinthians 12:2**

We only understand in part the mystery of Trinity and of God the Father sending His only begotten Son to be made flesh. Now we are adding to our understanding concerning the Father sending the Holy Spirit into earth at the request of Jesus. We only understand this, too, in part. What we partially understand is the parts are identifiable, separable, and sendable, yet one God.

THE HOLY SPIRIT IS SENT

Jesus was sent by the Father. Jesus Himself informed us of this when He said, *"...He gave His only begotten Son, that whoever believes in Him should not perish but have everlasting life. For God did not send His Son into the world to condemn the world, but that the world through Him might be saved..."* **John 3:16,17**. The Father sent His Son but it is also important to understand the Son yielded to being sent. According to the wisdom God spoke through Amos (see **Amos 3:3**), Jesus was in agreement with the Father's sending Him, or He would not have been able to have walked together with the Father.

The moment Jesus yielded to being sent by the Father, even though He was in agreement with being sent, He became subject to the Father's will. The one sent is subject to the will of the one sending. That is why Jesus constantly spoke the words, *"...I have come to do the will of the One who sent Me...".*

In the same way, the Father is sending the Holy Spirit. That means the Holy Spirit will be subject to the will of the Father. Whatever the Father wills, the Holy Spirit will eagerly carry it out because He has yielded to being sent by the Father. He is submitted because He is one with the Father and in agreement with the Father's plan. Even in the simplicity of these statements we can only understand in part. One Triune God, made up of three parts, identifiable, separable, and sendable. All of this is mysterious and only partially under-standable!

From only three verses, *John 14:15-17*, we have gained a profound understanding about the person and ministry of the Holy Spirit. We have learned:

1. Jesus loved the Church and interceded to the Father on behalf of the Church for the Holy Spirit to be sent to help us.

2. The Father sent the Holy Spirit as a gift to the Church because Jesus interceded on our behalf.

3. The Holy Spirit, in yielding to be sent by the Father, will be submitted to do the will of the Father on our behalf.

Now with great anticipation we will consider Jesus' words in the remainder of John chapters fourteen, fifteen, and sixteen, to look at the Father's will for the Holy Spirit in relation to us as believers.

THE HOLY SPIRIT & BELIEVERS

Look again at *John 14:15-17*. Verse sixteen tells us the Helper, who verse twenty-six tells us is the Holy Spirit, is going to abide with the disciples forever. The Holy Spirit is not going to come and go. Rather He is going to come and abide with us. Think of the wonder of the abiding presence of God the Holy Spirit!

Verse seventeen says *"...the world cannot receive Him because it neither sees Him nor knows Him..."*. Now Jesus is going to speak another mystery. *"But"*, Jesus says, *"You know Him, for He dwells with you and will be in you."* When the Holy Spirit comes as a gift from the Father in response to Jesus' prayer, the covenant relationship with the disciples will change. He will no longer simply dwell with the disciples, He will abide in them. God the Holy Spirit as a gift from God the Father will abide within each believer who receives Him as a gift!

We can be like Solomon in his Temple dedication prayer (see *II Chronicles 6:12-42*) and ask, "We know Lord Jesus you said the Holy Spirit will abide within us, but heaven and the heaven of heavens cannot contain Him. How can He dwell in our physical body?" Or we can accept Jesus' words as divine and believe with God all things are possible! If our omnipotent God wants the Holy Spirit to dwell within us as a gift to help us, then, instead of trying to understand with our natural man, we should receive with our spirit and accept by faith. God the Holy Spirit is going to live in the believer! Now we must determine what He is going to do from within His new dwelling place.

HOLY SPIRIT AS ADVOCATE AND COMFORTER

As Jesus verbally introduces the Holy Spirit to the disciples, He uses three names to refer to Him. He refers to Him as the Helper, the Spirit of truth, and the Holy Spirit. Each name helps us focus on some particular aspect of the Holy Spirit's character and ministry to us. We must consider the use and meaning of the word *"...Helper..."* from a translation perspective before we can consider its significance in reference to the Holy Spirit.

> *"16   ...I will pray the Father, and He will give you another Helper (Strong's Concordance number (3875)..."*
> **John 14:16**

> *"26   ...the Helper (3875), the Holy Spirit, whom the Father will send..."* **John 14:26**

> *"26 ...when the Helper (3875) comes, whom I shall send to you from the Father, the Spirit of truth..."* **John 15:26**

> *"7 ...if I do not go away, the Helper (3875) will not come to you..."* **John 16:7**

The New King James version of the Bible translates the Greek word listed as number **3875** in Strong's Concordance, as *'...helper...'*. Strong's Exhaustive Concordance of the Bible is keyed to the King James version of the Bible whose translators used the English word *"...comforter..."* instead of *"...helper..."*. The English listing in Strong's Concordance is *"...comforter..."* not *"...helper..."*. Strong's "Greek Dictionary of the New Testament" defines the Greek word listed as number 3875.

3875 *parakletos* - an intercessor, consoler: -- advocate, comforter.

Webster's New Universal Unabridged Dictionary defines **advocate**, **comforter**, and **comfort**.

advocate - 1. One who pleads the cause of another in a court of law; a counsel or counselor. 2. One who defends, vindicates, or espouses a cause by argument; one who is friendly to; an upholder; a defender.

comforter - A person or thing that comforts.

comfort - 1. To strengthen; to invigorate; to cheer or enliven. 2. To soothe in distress or sorrow; to ease the misery or grief of; to bring consolation or hope to. 1. relief from pain, grief, distress, etc. 2. A state of ease and quiet enjoyment, free from worry, pain, etc. 3. A person or thing that comforts. 4. Anything that makes life easy and comfortable. 5. In law, support; assistance; countenance; encouragement.

By referring to the Holy Spirit as *"...the Helper..."*, Jesus is signifying the Holy Spirit's ministry to us as believers will be as advocate and comforter. In other words, the Holy Spirit will plead our cause in the court of heaven. He will be our counselor to help defend and vindicate us. When the accuser of the brethren attacks us, the Holy Spirit will counsel us with an unbeatable case to defeat the attack the enemy brings against us. In short, He is sent by the Father to help us win!

As comforter He will strengthen, invigorate, cheer, and enliven us. He will soothe us in distress and sorrow. He will bring consolation and hope to us. His ministry will provide relief from pain, grief, distress, and similar attacks. He will help to insure us a state of ease and quiet enjoyment in the spirit, free from worry. He is sent by the Father to help us enjoy the life Jesus died to provide!

Each time we consider a ministry of the Holy Spirit to us as believers, we will rehearse what we have already learned. The Holy Spirit is sent by the Father and therefore totally submitted to do the Father's will on our behalf because the Father wills it. We are also confident the Holy Spirit is in agreement with the Father's will because we know He is one with the Father, and two cannot walk together except they be agreed. With the Holy Spirit submitted and eager to do the Father's will, He will fulfill His ministry as *'parakletos'* to us!

THE HOLY SPIRIT AS TEACHER

Jesus tells His disciples the Holy Spirit is going to be our teacher.

> *"26 The Helper, the Holy Spirit, whom the Father will send in My name, He will teach you all things..."*
> ***John 14:26***

In his letter to the church at Corinth Paul also wrote of this aspect of the Holy Spirit's ministry. He wrote,

> *"9 Eye has not seen nor ear heard, Nor have entered into the heart of man the things which God has prepared for those who love Him. 10 But God has revealed them to us through His Spirit. For the Spirit searches all things, yes, the deep things of God. 11 For what man knows the things of a man except the spirit of the man which is in him? Even so no one knows the things of God except the Spirit of God. 12 Now we have received, not the spirit of the world, but the Spirit who is from God, that we might know the things that have been freely given to us by God. 13 These things we also speak, not in words which man's wisdom teaches but which the Holy Spirit teaches, comparing spiritual things with spiritual. 14 But the natural man does not receive the things of the Spirit of God, for they are foolishness to him; nor can he know them, because they are spiritually discerned. 15 But he who is spiritual judges all things, yet he himself is rightly judged by no one. 16 For who has known the mind of the Lord that he may instruct Him? But we have the mind of Christ."* ***I Corinthians 2:9-16***

To understand this revelation the Holy Spirit has inspired Paul to use a comparison of natural *heard, nor have entered into the heart of man the things which God has prepared for those who love Him. But God has revealed them to us through His Spirit. For the Spirit searches all things, yes, the deep things of God.*". In the first part of verse eleven he asks, *"For what man knows the things of a man except the spirit of the man which is in him"?*

In other words, you cannot know the condition of another man just by looking, listening, or considering with natural understanding. You may see the man smiling and saying he is doing fine. You may think, based on what you have seen and heard, the man is doing fine. However, the man may actually be in terrible condition hiding behind smiles and pleasantries. Unless the spirit of the man tells you his condition from his heart, or unless the Holy Spirit reveals it, you cannot know it.

In the last half of verse eleven Paul makes the comparison between the natural illustration of man and God Himself. He says, *"Even so no one knows the things of God except the Spirit of God."*. In other words, just like you cannot know the condition of another man, you cannot know the things of God just by looking, listening, or considering with natural understanding. It is only through the Spirit of God that God reveals to us what is in His own heart.

Paul wrote in verses twelve and thirteen, *"Now we have received, not the spirit of the world, but the Spirit who is from God, that we might know the things that have been freely given to us by God"*. When the Holy Spirit searches the deep things of God, He is searching the things that have been freely given to us by God. Scripture teaches God has given us all things that pertain to life and godliness. Scripture also teaches out of the heart flow the issues of life.

> *"2 Grace and peace be multiplied to you in the knowledge of God and of Jesus our Lord, 3 as His divine power has given to us all things that pertain to life and godliness, through the knowledge of Him who called us by glory and virtue, 4 by which have been given to us exceedingly great and precious promises, that through these you may be partakers of the divine nature, having escaped the corruption that is in the world through lust."*
> **II Peter 1:2**

"23 Keep your heart with all diligence, for out of it spring the issues of life." **Proverbs 4:23**

When the Holy Spirit searches the heart of God on our behalf, He is searching for the issues that pertain to life and godliness. Paul wrote in *I Corinthians 2:13*, *"These things we also speak, not in words which man's wisdom teaches but which the Holy Spirit teaches, comparing spiritual things with spiritual"*. The ministry of the Holy Spirit revealing the heart of God is in a teaching format in order that we may be able to grow in knowledge and understanding of God. It is as we learn through His teaching ministry that grace and peace will be multiplied, we will receive as a practical part of our lives all things that pertain to life and godliness, and we will actually walk in the ability of His divine nature.

We must consider one other important aspect of the Holy Spirit's ministry in order to be effectively taught by Him. *I Corinthians 2:14* tells us, *"the natural man does not receive the things of the Spirit of God, for they are foolishness to him; nor can he know them, because they are spiritually discerned"*. The Holy Spirit's ministry is not to our intellect or our natural mind but to our spirit. This applies to all of the Holy Spirit's ministries not just teaching.

THE HOLY SPIRIT AS SUPERNATURAL MEMORY

The failure of the old covenant was the weakness of the flesh. Man could not keep covenant in his own ability. So God gave man a new covenant. The difference between the new covenant and the old covenant is fundamentally simple. The old covenant was in man's ability. The new covenant is in God's ability. That means God has made a way for us to live in covenant with Him in His ability. The entire new covenant is based on the ability of God not the ability of man. Man simply must be willing to receive the ability of God as a free gift so that all boasting will be only in God.

> *"8 For by grace you have been saved through faith, and that not of yourselves; it is the gift of God, 9 not of works, lest anyone should boast."* **Ephesians 2:8,9**

Every aspect of the new covenant is designed to be in the ability of God. Whether study of the Word, learning, healing the sick, or any other aspect of life in the new covenant, everything is to be in the ability of God. Many times we get caught up in dead works, works done in our own ability, and lose the peace and joy of the Lord. One such area is memorization of scripture and revelation. This is an area in which the enemy has deceived many people keeping them from growth in the spirit. They have much knowledge of scripture, but this knowledge came through their own ability causing them to be puffed up rather than mature.

We do not learn the things of the spirit because we have a high IQ but because we are open to the Holy Spirit to teach us. We do not memorize scripture nor try to hold on to revelation knowledge in the power of our own intellect but in the ability of the Holy Spirit. Look at Jesus' words to his disciples in this matter.

"26 The Helper, the Holy Spirit, whom the Father will send in My name, He will teach you all things, and bring to your remembrance all things that I said to you."
John 14:26

Over the years I have counseled and ministered to many people who have let the enemy rob them of this great blessing. Perhaps the most dramatic illustration happened to a young man who cut his hand fairly badly. The wound was bleeding heavily and he fretted outloud, "Oh no, I can't remember where the scripture is in Ezekiel that stops bleeding"!

This has been the plight of many well meaning Christians. Subtly the enemy has turned them from the new covenant back again to the old covenant. They try to rely on their ability and their memory to make the covenant work. The power of the new covenant for our lives is the ability of God. Instead of trying to remember the scripture to stop the bleeding, the young man should have called on the Holy Spirit to help him. If it was scripture the young man needed to remember, the Holy Spirit would have brought it back to his remembrance.

Reliance on God and not our own selves is the simplicity of the gospel. The Holy Spirit *"...bringing to our remembrance all things Christ said to us..."* is His job. He is submitted to the Father's will to fulfill this aspect of His ministry. Let us stop trying to take His place in our own ability and let Him do His job. He will bring to our remembrance all things Christ has said to us. That is the Father's will. Our part is to call on Him according to the Father's will and receive His ministry.

THE HOLY SPIRIT AS WITNESS

"26 But when the Helper comes, whom I shall send to you from the Father, the Spirit of truth who proceeds from the Father, He will testify of Me. 27 And you also will bear witness, because you have been with Me from the beginning." **John 15:26,27**

Jesus is instructing His disciples here regarding the person and ministry of the Holy Spirit in relation to them as believers. He is telling them the Holy Spirit will give them testimony of Jesus. In a court of law a person who gives testimony is referred to as a witness. A witness gives testimony of what he has seen, heard, or been involved personally. Valid testimony cannot be based on hearsay, rumor, or other similar uninvolved activities. The witness must have been personally involved in seeing, hearing, or the actions to which he is giving testimony.

In order for the Holy Spirit to give valid testimony of Jesus, He can only testify of what He has seen, heard, or been involved with Jesus. Imagine the eternal, omnipotent Triune God giving us testimony of Himself through one of His parts, God the Holy Spirit. Consider the personal involvement of the Holy Spirit with the Father and the Son throughout eternity. His testimony will be perfect and true as the Spirit of Truth conveying accurately those things the Father and Son desire to reveal to us.

To help us better understand the ministry of the Holy Spirit as witness, we can use our natural courtroom illustration again. In a court of law a witness, no matter how credible, does not enter the courtroom and immediately begin testifying on his own accord. Instead He is called, introduced, sworn in, examined, then cross-examined by the proper authorities. The examination takes place in the form of specific questions being asked of the witness, examining the witness regarding his knowledge of the case at hand.

The Holy Spirit's ministry as witness operates similarly. Even though He has come to abide within us, He does not immediately begin testifying on His own accord. Instead, He must be called upon by the believer. Understanding of this simple truth is essential for the believer to most effectively benefit from the Holy Spirit's ministry.

Let us compare Jesus' ministry regarding man calling on Him for salvation. Do you remember what Paul wrote to the church at Rome?

> *"13 Whoever calls on the name of the Lord shall be saved. 14 How then shall they call on Him in whom they have not believed? And how shall they believe in Him of whom they have not heard? And how shall they hear without a preacher? 15 And how shall they preach unless they are sent? As it is written: "How beautiful are the feet of those who preach the gospel of peace, who bring glad tidings of good things!" 16 But they have not all obeyed the gospel. For Isaiah says, Lord, who has believed our report? 17 So then faith comes by hearing and hearing by the word of God."* **Romans 10:13-17**

It is the will of God for all mankind to be saved, but Jesus' ministry of salvation does not work automatically in our lives. We must *"...call on the name of the Lord..."* to be saved.

God's holy plan requires that *"...by grace you have been saved through faith, and that not of yourselves; it is the gift of God, not of works, lest anyone should boast..."*. For us to benefit from Jesus' ministry of salvation, we must call on the Lord. In order to do that, we must believe in Jesus as Lord. In order to believe, we must hear of Jesus. In order to hear someone must tell us. In order for someone to tell us, they must be sent. So faith to believe in Jesus for us to call on Him in order to be saved comes from the Word being ministered to us by someone sent to tell us of Jesus' ministry of salvation.

God has a will for the Holy Spirit to minister to us as believers. As a rule the Holy Spirit's ministry does not operate automatically to us. (There are exceptions to this rule but we must consider the rule rather than the exceptions.) For us to most effectively benefit from the Holy Spirit's ministries we must call on Him in whatever area we need ministry. In order to do that, we must believe the Father has sent the Holy Spirit to minister to us according to His will just like He sent Jesus to minister to us according to His will. In order for us to believe, we must hear of the Holy Spirit and the ministries the Father has willed for Him to have on our behalf. In order for us to hear, someone must tell us. In order for someone to tell us, they must be sent. So faith to call on the person and ministry of the Holy Spirit comes from the Word being ministered to us by someone sent to tell us of the Holy Spirit and His ministries. This principle of calling on the person and ministry of the Holy Spirit applies to all of the Holy Spirit's ministries including that of witness.

THE HOLY SPIRIT AS GUIDE

> *"13 When He, the Spirit of truth, has come, He will guide you into all truth; for He will not speak on His own authority, but whatever He hears He will speak; and He will tell you things to come. 14 He will glorify Me, for He will take of what is Mine and declare it to you. 15 All things that the Father has are Mine. Therefore I said that He will take of Mine and declare it to you."*
> *John 16:13-15*

By now we are able to identify the Holy Spirit from three names, Helper, Spirit of Truth, or Holy Spirit. We have already seen Jesus use three names to reinforce our understanding of certain aspects of the Holy Spirit's ministry to us. We see in *John 16:13* the Holy Spirit as the Spirit of Truth *"...will guide you into all truth...".* Webster's New Universal Unabridged Dictionary defines **guide**.

> **guide** - to point out the way for; to direct on a course; conduct; lead.

The Father has willed for the Holy Spirit to be our guide. He will lead us in many different areas of life such as vocation, marriage, place to live, and many other areas. However, a point of profound significance to our successful relationship with the Holy Spirit must be made here. The Holy Spirit's primary responsibility as guide is to guide us into all truth. Jesus said of Himself that He is truth.

> *"6 Jesus said to him (Thomas), 'I am the way, the truth, and the life. No one comes to the Father except through Me."*
> *John 14:6*

104

The Holy Spirit's primary responsibility as guide is to guide us into Christ!

Paul wrote to the church at Rome, *"as many as are led by the Spirit of God, these are sons of God"* **Romans 8:14**. Most believers have understood they are supposed to be led by the Holy Spirit. However, most have not understood the primary leading responsibility of the Holy Spirit is to guide them into Christ. The lack of knowledge and understanding has opened the door for the enemy to deceive many. Paul told the church at Corinth to beware of *"...false apostles, deceitful workers, transforming themselves into apostles of Christ. And no wonder! For Satan himself transforms into an angel of light..."* **II Corinthians 11:13,14**. The enemy will deceive all whom he is able to deceive. He can only deceive those who lack proper knowledge of the will of God.

In nearly twenty years of ministry in approximately forty nations I have seen many believers deceived by the enemy in the name of following the leading of the Holy Spirit. These people do not demonstrate Christ-like character or the fruit of the spirit, but they can tell you what the spirit has told them about your life or someone else's life but never their own. They have opened the door for a wrong spirit to lead them into a life of destruction.

The Holy Spirit will not violate His prime directive to guide us into Christ. He is most concerned that we individually have life eternal. Jesus told us *"...this is life eternal, that they may know You, the only true God, and Jesus Christ whom You have sent"* **John 17:3**. The Holy Spirit is commissioned by the Father to guide us into all truth. Certainly that involves truth in all areas but primarily Christ as truth. If a believer does not understand this, they will be more open to the juicy morsels the enemy will feed them about others. Of course the enemy disguises himself as the spirit of light and truth in order to deceive.

John told the church in his first epistle to test the spirits.

> *"1 Beloved, do not believe every spirit, but test the spirits, whether they are of God; because many false prophets have gone out into the world. 2 By this you know the Spirit of God: Every spirit that confesses that Jesus Christ has come in the flesh is of God, 3 and every spirit that does not confess that Jesus Christ has come in the flesh is not of God. And this is the spirit of the Antichrist, which you have heard was coming, and is now already in the world. 4 You are of God, little children, and have overcome them, because He who is in you is greater than he who is in the world. 5 They are of the world. Therefore they speak as of the world, and the world hears them. 6 We are of God. He who knows God hears us; he who is not of God does not hear us. By this we know the spirit of truth and the spirit of error." I John 4:1-6*

He is writing of false prophets in the earth, but his main emphasis is on the spirits who motivate the false prophets. One of the simplest tests with which to test the spirits is whether the spirit is leading me into Christ as His primary guidance. If the spirit has told you what God wants for everyone else and how to straighten out the church but the spirit to whom you are listening is not speaking to you about your own life, then you are listening to the wrong spirit.

The Holy Spirit desires to guide you into all truth so you may experience life. Then out of the life you have experienced, you can share it with others. Jesus established this as a principle of life in the kingdom of God when He sent the twelve disciples out to minister. He told them, *"freely you have received, freely give"* **Matthew 10:8**.

THE HOLY SPIRIT AS CONVINCER

Up to this point we have considered the person and ministry of the Holy Spirit exclusively to the Church. Before we conclude this chapter regarding the ministry of the Holy Spirit, we must include one aspect of His ministry to the world. We will see even this aspect of His ministry to the world involves us as the Church.

> *"5 But now I go away to Him who sent Me, and none of you asks Me, 'Where are You going?' 6 But because I have said these things to you, sorrow has filled your heart. 7 Nevertheless I tell you the truth. It is to your advantage that I go away; for if I do not go away, the Helper will not come to you; but if I depart, I will send Him to you. 8 And when He has come, He will convict the world of sin, and of righteousness, and of judgment: 9 of sin, because they do not believe in Me; 10 of righteousness, because I go to My Father and you see Me no more; 11 of judgment, because the ruler of this world is judged."*
>
> **John 16:5-11**

Jesus is telling us the Holy Spirit as the Helper *"will convict the world of sin, of righteousness, and of judgment"*. Notice how Jesus used the name ***"Helper"*** referring to the Holy Spirit in giving the disciples these instructions. This name has been used by Jesus to refer to the Holy Spirit in relation to the Church in previous portions of scripture. Calling the Holy

Spirit *"Helper"* reinforces our understanding of certain aspects of His ministry to us. In other words He is sent to **"Help"** us.

In order to understand how the Holy Spirit convicting the world of sin, of righteousness, and of judgment helps the Church, we must turn again to Paul's letter to the church at Rome. Without quoting the entire portion of scripture we will simply rehearse the gist of **Romans 10:13-17**. Anyone who calls on the name of the Lord will be saved. However, in order for them to call on the Lord, we have seen certain requirements must be met first: believing in the Lord, hearing of the Lord, someone preaching of Jesus to them, the preacher being sent to them, and their obtaining faith from the Word they have heard.

The Holy Spirit will convict the world of sin, of righteousness, and of judgment so the world may be saved. Jesus told us *"...God did not send His Son into the world to condemn the world, but that the world through Him might be saved"* **John 3:17**. The conviction the Holy Spirit brings is to produce salvation not condemnation. The world can only be saved by *"...calling on the name of the Lord..."*. Paul told the church at Corinth *"...no one can say that Jesus is Lord except by the Holy Spirit..."* **I Corinthians 12:3**.

Now for understanding in this matter. The Father has sent the Church into all the world to preach the gospel to every creature that the world may hear of Christ in order to be saved. As the Church testifies of Jesus to the world, the Holy Spirit works together with us as Helper to convict the world of sin, of righteousness, and of judgment. The Holy Spirit convicts the world *"...of sin, because they do not believe in Me..."* **John 16:9**. In other words, the Holy Spirit convicts the world that it would be a sin unto death to reject Jesus as Lord and Savior. The Holy Spirit convicts the world *"...of righteousness, because I go to My Father and you see Me no more..."* **John 16:10**. In other words, the Holy Spirit convinces the world that Jesus has been made the righteous Lord of Lords seated at the right hand of the Father. The Holy Spirit convicts the world *"...of judgment, because the ruler of this world is judged..."* **John 16:11**. In other words, the Holy Spirit convinces the world that life under the rulers of this world is doomed because they have been judged as authors of death rather than life (The rulers of this world refer to spirit rulers of Satan's kingdom rather than natural rulers. See **Ephesians 6:10-20**, **Colossians 2:11-23**, and **Hebrews 2:14-18**).

We can see this cooperative ministry between the Church and the Holy Spirit to the world written of by Luke on the day of Pentecost. When the Day of Pentecost had fully come and the Holy Spirit had come to the Church, Jerusalem was in an uproar. Jews from every nation under heaven heard the sound of the Holy Spirit and came to see this spectacle. They argued among themselves as to exactly what was happening. Then Peter stood and began to minister the Word to them. He spoke of Old Testament prophecy regarding the last days' outpouring of the Holy Spirit and of the salvation of mankind through the Lord Jesus. He spoke of the Jews' relationship with Jesus during His earthly ministry. Luke records the final confrontation between Peter and the Jews that day.

> *"36 Therefore let all the house of Israel know assuredly that God has made this Jesus, whom you crucified, both Lord and Christ. 37 Now when they heard this, they were cut to the heart, and said to Peter and the rest of the apostles, 'Men and brethren, what shall we do?' 38 Then Peter said to them, Repent, and let every one of you be baptized in the name of Jesus Christ for the remission of sins; and you shall receive the gift of the Holy Spirit. 39 For the promise is to you and to your children, and to all who are afar off, as many as the Lord our God will call."*
>
> **Acts 2:36-39**

According to what Jesus already told us in ***John 16:7-11**,* the convicting ministry of the Holy Spirit to the world was to begin only after Jesus had gone away to the Father. The Day of Pentecost marked the beginning of a new ministry for the Holy Spirit to the Church and to the world.

Peter ministered to the same Jews who had rejected and crucified Jesus. Peter's ministry was successful to bring approximately three thousand of them to a place of repentance and salvation that day. His success was primarily a result of the new ministry of the Holy Spirit to convict the world of sin, of righteousness, and of judgment.

As we go forth into all the world to proclaim the good news, we do not go alone nor in our own strength. We will have the Holy Spirit as our Helper to give us the ability to preach the gospel. As we preach, we give Him the opportunity to convict those to whom we minister of sin, of righteousness, and of judgment through the Word we speak to the world.

Chapter Six

RECEIVING MINISTRY FROM THE HOLY SPIRIT

Receiving ministry from the Holy Spirit is what we do when He ministers to us. Before we can find out how we receive ministry from Him, we need to see how He ministers to us. We have already seen throughout the course of discovery in chapters fourteen, fifteen, and sixteen of John's gospel the primary relationship the believer has with the Holy Spirit in the new covenant is internal rather than external. That is not to say He cannot minister to us externally, but His primary ministry to us as individual believers is from His indwelling presence. Even when external ministry comes to us, He must still give revelation of that ministry to our inner man.

We have already considered the Holy Spirit's inspiration to Paul emphasizing this point, by saying, *"...the natural man does not receive the things of the Spirit of God, for they are foolishness to him; nor can he know them, because they are spiritually discerned" I Corinthians 2:14.* **The Holy Spirit's ministry is to our spirit!** Whether He comforts, teaches, brings to our remembrance, testifies, or guides us, His ministry is to our inner man. Knowing where the Holy Spirit ministers to us, internally to our spirit, "sets the stage" for us to find out how He ministers to us.

It is not until chapter sixteen, the last of the three chapters of John's gospel we are using as scriptural foundation for revelation on the person and ministry of the Holy Spirit, that we receive clearest understanding in how He ministers to us.

> *"13 However, when He, the Spirit of truth, has come, He will guide you into all truth; for He will not speak on His own authority, but whatever He hears He will speak; and He will tell you things to come. 14 He will glorify Me, for He will take of what is Mine and declare it to you. 15 All things that the Father has are Mine. Therefore I said that He will take of Mine and declare it to you."*
>
> **John 16:13-15**

Jesus says plainly in verse thirteen the Holy Spirit *"will not speak on His own authority, but whatever He hears He will speak"*. The mode of communication about which Jesus speaks most clearly regarding the Holy Spirit's ministry to us is speech. Whatever the Holy Spirit hears from Jesus and the Father, He will speak to us. This process of communication takes place in our inner man, in our spirit, not our natural ears nor our natural intellect.

THE HOLY SPIRIT SPEAKS

Let us examine *"...speak..."* more closely. Strong's Exhaustive Concordance of the Bible numbers the English word *"...speak..."*, used in John 16:13, as number **2980**. Strong's "Greek Dictionary of the New Testament" defines the Greek word listed as number 2980.

> **2980 *laleo*** a prol. form of an otherwise obsol. verb; to talk, i.e. utter words: — preach, say, speak (after), talk, tell, utter.

Webster's New Universal Unabridged Dictionary defines the English word *"...speak..."*.

> 1. to utter words or articulate sounds in the ordinary voice; to talk. 2. to make a speech; to deliver an address or lecture; to discourse. 3. to express or communicate opinions, feelings, ideas, etc. by or as by talking. 4. to make mention; to tell by speech or writing. 5. to make or emit sound; to sound. 6. to communicate orally with another or others; to converse.

> 1. to utter with the mouth; to pronounce; to utter articulately, as human beings. 2. to tell; to say; to make known by or as by speaking; to declare; to announce. 3. to proclaim; to celebrate; declare or show to be. 4. to use or be able to use (a given language) in speaking. 5. to address; to speak to. 6. in nautical usage, to hail (a ship).

The English word *"...speak..."* and the Greek word *"...laleo..."* convey the same basic meaning, **to communicate by uttering words**. Even though the Holy Spirit's ministry to us is in the spirit rather than the natural, Jesus' instructions concerning the Holy Spirit's ministry used this Greek word *"...laleo..."*, translated *"...speak..."* in English. That means, in *John 16:13*, the Holy Spirit is going to communicate to our inner man by uttering words to our spirit.

To limit the infinite God would be carnal natural thought. To say the only way God the Holy Spirit ministers to us as believers is by uttering words to our spirit would be wrong. God communicates to us through a wide variety of means as He chooses.

In considering the communication process of speech, about which Jesus wrote in **John 16:13**, we are considering only one way the Holy Spirit ministers to us as believers. However, because this is the communication method of which Jesus spoke most understandably in His instructions regarding the ministry of the Holy Spirit in chapters fourteen, fifteen, and sixteen of John's gospel, we would be foolish not to consider it carefully.

Jesus said the Holy Spirit would...

"...teach you all things..." **John 14:26**,

"...bring to your remembrance all things that I said to you..." **John 14:26**,

"...testify of Me..." **John 15:26**,

"...convict the world of sin, and of righteousness, and of judgment..." **John 16:8**,

"...guide you into all truth..." **John 16:13**,

"...glorify Me, for He will take of what is Mine and declare it to you..." **John 16:14.**

We understand what the English words *"teach"*, *"bring to your remembrance"*, *"testify"*, *"convict"*, *"guide"*, and *"glorify"* mean. Yet these are not as simply and clearly understandable as Jesus' words *"...He will not speak on His own authority, but whatever He hears He will speak..."* **John 16:13**.

From His internal dwelling place the Holy Spirit is going to speak to our spirit. That is simple, direct, and fundamentally understandable. Our main objective in this book is to explore this speaking form of communication from the Holy Spirit.

HEARING HIS VOICE

Websters New Universal Unabridged Dictionary defines **communication**.

> 1. the act of imparting, conferring, or delivering, from one to another. 2. intercourse by words, letters, or messages; interchange of thoughts or opinions, by conference or other means. 3. the science and art of communicating as a branch of study. 4. means of communicating; specifically, (a) connecting passage; means of passing from place to place; (b) a system for sending and receiving messages, as by telephone, telegraph, radio, etc.; (c) a system for moving troops and material. 5. that which is communicated or imparted; information or intelligence imparted by word or writing.

Communication is not just sending information, it also involves receiving the information sent. If the form of communication used is speaking, then the person to whom spoken must hear the speech for there to be communication between the two parties. The process of communication requires both speaking and hearing to be complete.

The form of communication we are considering from the Holy Spirit is speaking. Because He is going to speak to us, then we must be able to hear His voice for the process of

communication to be complete. When the Holy Spirit ministers to us by speaking to us, we must be able to hear His voice
in order to receive ministry from Him.

PREVAILING FEAR

Before we proceed any further in our search for understanding how to receive ministry from the Holy Spirit, we must
remove a hindrance. ***Jesus*** told us there is a thief loose in the
earth who *"...does not come except to steal, and to kill, and to
destroy..."* ***John 10:10****. **Paul*** told us we are to stand against
the wiles of the devil because *"...we do not wrestle against
flesh and blood, but against principalities, against powers,
against the rulers of the darkness of this age, against spiritual
hosts of wickedness in the heavenly places"* ***Ephesians 6:12****.
John* told us *"...do not believe every spirit, but test the spirits,
whether they are of God; because many false prophets have
gone out into the world..."* ***I John 4:1****.

There is a fear prevailing in the Body of Christ regarding hearing voices in the spirit. Many are so afraid they will be
led astray by voices from wrong spirits, they are unwilling to
hear the voice of any spirit. Essentially this closes the door on
a believer successfully walking in the spirit. This fear is a
mountain of hindrance holding back the Church of the Lord
Jesus in the earth! It must be removed. All hindrances or
obstacles are removed with the Word of the Lord. We must
receive knowledge and understanding of the Word regarding
the will of the Lord in this matter in order to have this hindrance
removed from our lives. The Church must learn to hear in the
spirit!

LIFE IN THE SPIRIT

Firstly, let us consider the need for hearing in the spirit. Life in the natural world involves the five senses of sight, smell, taste, touch, and hearing. Even though each healthy child is born with these five senses, they must be developed in order for the child to live successfully in the earth. If only one of the five senses is impaired or missing in the child's life, such as sight, it decreases the child's opportunity for success as God intended him to live. So too, it is in the spiritual world. We are born again into the spiritual world with spiritual senses. However, just like in the natural, they must be developed in order for us to live successfully in the spirit.

During Paul's "house arrest" in Rome he had opportunity to minister to many Jews. One day he called the leaders of the Jews together and began speaking to them about his arrest. In the course of conversation he began to teach them concerning Jesus from the Law of Moses and the Prophets. Some believed and some did not. When they began to disagree among themselves, Paul quoted a word the Holy Spirit had spoken about them through Isaiah the prophet.

> *"26 Go to this people and say: Hearing you will hear, and shall not understand; and seeing you will see, and not perceive; 27 For the hearts of this people have grown dull. Their ears are hard of hearing, and their eyes they have closed, lest they should see with their eyes and hear with their ears, lest they should understand with their hearts and turn, so that I should heal them."* **Acts 28:26,27**

Paul was not saying they were naturally blind, deaf, and ignorant. Rather he was saying they could not see, hear, nor understand with their inner man in the spirit. Their spiritual senses were not functioning for them to see, hear, and understand in the spirit. In Paul's letter to the church at Corinth he explained very carefully why the Jews could not see, hear nor understand in the spirit.

> *"15 Even to this day, when Moses is read a veil lies on their heart. 16 Nevertheless when one turns to the Lord, the veil is taken away."* **II Corinthians 2:15,16**

Their spiritual senses were not working because their heart was not turned to God. The result was they missed the life God intended them to have through Christ in the spirit.

In almost all of Paul's writings the Holy Spirit inspired him to speak on the requirement for the Christian to live and walk in the spirit. The most straightforward of his writings in this matter was to the church at Galatia.

> *"16 I say then: Walk in the spirit, and you shall not fulfill the lust of the flesh. 17 For the flesh lusts against the spirit, and the spirit against the flesh; and these are contrary to one another, so that you do not do the things that you wish. 18 but if you are led by the Spirit, you are not under the law. 19 Now the works of the flesh are evident, which are: adultery, fornication, uncleanness, lewdness, 20 envy, murders, drunkenness, revelries, and the like; of which I tell you beforehand, just as I also told you in time past, that those who practice such things will not inherit the kingdom of God. 22 but the fruit of the spirit is love, joy, peace, longsuffering, kindness, goodness, faithfulness, 23 gentleness, self-control. Against such there is no law. 24 And those who are Christ's have crucified the flesh with its passions and desires. 25 If we live in the spirit, let us also walk in the spirit."*
> **Galatians 5:16-25**

He is emphatically telling those who are Christ's to *"...walk in the spirit..."!* This is not an option for special reward when we get to heaven. The alternative to not walking in the spirit is walking in the flesh. Those who walk in the flesh *"...will not inherit the kingdom of God...".* Paul tells us *"...the kingdom of God is not eating and drinking, but righteousness and peace and joy in the Holy Spirit..." **Romans 14:17***. We must walk in the spirit in order to inherit righteousness, peace, and joy in the Holy Spirit.

Through Paul's letter to the church at Corinth we have already seen how *"...the natural man does not receive the things of the Spirit of God, for they are foolishness to him; nor can he know them, because they are spiritually discerned..." **I Corinthians 2:14***. Life in Christ is not according to our natural seeing, hearing, nor understanding but according to what we see, hear, and understand in the spirit.

Jesus was ministering to some of the Pharisees one day on the true shepherd versus thieves, murderers, and hirelings. He was using the natural illustration of sheep and shepherd to give the Pharisees an opportunity to compare what He was teaching regarding spiritual matters with what they already knew in the natural.

> *"1 Most assuredly, I say to you, he who does not enter the sheepfold by the door, but climbs up some other way, the same is a thief and a robber. 2 But he who enters by the door is the shepherd of the sheep. 3 To him the door-keeper opens, and the sheep hear his voice; and he calls his own sheep by name and leads them out. 4 And when he brings out his own sheep, he goes before them; and the sheep follow him, for they know his voice. 5 Yet they will*

119

by no means follow a stranger, but will flee from him, for they do not know the voice of strangers. 6 Jesus used this illustration, but they did not understand the things which He spoke to them. 7 Then Jesus said to them again, Most assuredly, I say to you, I am the door of the sheep. 8 All who ever came before Me are thieves and robbers, but the sheep did not hear them. 9 I am the door. If anyone enters by Me, he will be saved, and will go in and out and find pasture. 10 The thief does not come except to steal, and to kill, and to destroy. I have come that they may have life, and that they may have it more abundantly. 11 I am the good shepherd. The good shepherd gives His life for the sheep. 12 But a hireling, he who is not the shepherd, one who does not own the sheep, sees the wolf coming and leaves the sheep and flees; and the wolf catches the sheep and scatters them. 13 The hireling flees because he is a hireling and does not care about the sheep. 14 I am the good shepherd; and I know My sheep, and am known by My own. 15 As the Father knows Me, even so I know the Father; and I lay down My life for the sheep. 16 And other sheep I have which are not of this fold; them also I must bring, and they will hear My voice; and there will be one flock and one shepherd. 17 Therefore My Father loves Me, because I lay down My life that I may take it again. 18 No one takes it from Me, but I lay it down of Myself. I have power to lay it down, and I have power to take it again. This command I have received from My Father. 19 Therefore there was a division again among the Jews because of these sayings. 20 And many of them said, He has a demon and is mad. Why do you listen to Him? 21 Others said, These are not the words of one who has a demon. Can a demon open the eyes of the blind? 22 Now it was the Feast of Dedication in Jerusalem, and it was winter. 23 And Jesus walked in the temple, in Solomon's porch. 24 Then the Jews surrounded Him and said to Him, How long do You keep us in doubt? If You are the Christ, tell us plainly. 25 Jesus answered them, I told you, and you do not believe. the works that I do in My Father's name, they bear witness of Me. 26 But you do not believe, because you are not of My sheep, as I said to you. 27 My sheep hear My voice, and I know them, and they follow Me. 28 And I give them eternal life, and they shall never perish;

neither shall anyone snatch them out of My hand. 29 My Father, who has given them to Me, is greater than all; and no one is able to snatch them out of My Father's hand. 30 I and My Father are one." **John 10:1-30**

In verses three, four, sixteen, and twenty-seven Jesus says plainly **"...My sheep hear My voice..."**! Jesus is not speaking figuratively but plainly. It is also stated plainly that they follow Him in verses three, four, sixteen, and twenty seven. He means His sheep hear His voice so they may follow Him. Unless the sheep are able to hear the voice of their shepherd, they will not be able to follow Him.

Jesus also instructed His disciples about the ministry of the Holy Spirit as we have already begun considering in the beginning of this chapter. He told them *"...when He, the Spirit of truth, has come, He will guide you into all truth; for He will not speak on His own authority, but whatever He hears He will speak; and He will tell you things to come..."* **John 16:13**. We have also already learned His ministry is not to our natural man but to our spirit. Unless we are able to hear the voice of the Holy Spirit as the Spirit of truth, we will not be able to be guided into all truth.

The need for hearing in the spirit is clear in scripture. Unless believers understand they have spiritual senses and must develop them in order to live successfully in the spirit, they will try to live in Christ with their natural senses and miss the life God intended them to have while they still live on the earth. That was the problem the Jews had. They could see, hear, and understand with their natural senses, but they could not see, hear, and understand with their spiritual senses. Their hearts were not turned to God. Let us learn from their mistakes. Let us turn our hearts to the Lord and develop our spiritual senses, especially our ability to hear the voice of our Shepherd and of the Holy Spirit! With our hearts turned to the Lord and with the understanding the Holy Spirit's primary responsibility is to guide us into Christ our God will protect us from evil spirits.

> *"9 So I say to you, ask, and it will be given to you; seek, and you will find; knock, and it will be opened to you. 10 For everyone who asks receives, and he who seeks finds, and to him who knocks it will be opened. 11 If a son asks for bread from any father among you, will he give him a stone? Or if he asks for a fish, will he give him a serpent instead of a fish? 12 Or if he asks for an egg, will he offer him as scorpion? 13 If you then, being evil, know how to give good gifts to your children, how much more will your heavenly Father give the Holy Spirit to those who ask Him!"* **Luke 11:9-13**

HOW TO HEAR THE VOICE OF THE HOLY SPIRIT

Perhaps the revelation of the Trinity is the most mysterious of all. How can we understand the Triune God is three separable and identifiable parts yet only One God. Comparing natural things made up of three separable and identifiable parts will help with our understanding. We can compare such things as water, made up of $H2O$, two parts hydrogen and one part oxygen or man, made up of spirit, soul, and body. However, without divine intervention we will never understand the mysteries of God.

Demonstration of the separability and identifiability of the Trinity is probably the simplest to see in the portion of scripture when John baptized Jesus in the Jordan river.

"13 Then Jesus came from Galilee to John at the Jordan to be baptized by him. 14 And John tried to prevent Him, saying, "I need to be baptized by You, and are You coming to me?" 15 But Jesus answered and said to him, "Permit it to be so now, for thus it is fitting for us to fulfill all righteousness." Then he allowed Him. 16 When He had been baptized, Jesus came up immediately from the water; and behold, the heavens were opened to Him, and He saw the Spirit of God descending like a dove and alighting upon Him. 17 and suddenly a voice came from heaven, saying, "This is My beloved Son, in whom I am well pleased." **Matthew 3:13-17**

There stood the Word of God made flesh in the person of Jesus, the Spirit of God descending from heaven in appearance as a dove, and the Father God speaking in an audible voice for all to hear (see also *John 12:28* regarding the Father speaking in an audible voice for all to hear). Three separable and identifiable parts yet only one True God. What a divine mystery!

Our focus is on hearing the voice of the Holy Spirit. Even though our God is One, the voice of the Holy Spirit is a separable and identifiable part of the One True God. We accept the mystery of this truth and receive understanding in part to be able to view the person and ministry of the Holy Spirit and to learn to hear His voice.

When a person speaks to another, the person spoken to is hearing the voice of the one speaking. We have already seen the word "speak" defined as, "to communicate by uttering words". That means when a person speaks they are uttering words as their part of the process of communication. For the communication to be complete the person spoken to must receive the words uttered.

"Uttering words" is the same thing as saying "giving utter-ance". "Receiving the words uttered" is the same thing as saying "receiving utterance".

SPEAKING = GIVING UTTERANCE

HEARING = RECEIVING UTTERANCE

THE DAY OF PENTECOST

Now look at our first real clue to breakthrough in understanding the process of communication between the Holy Spirit and believers involving speaking and hearing. We find it recorded by Luke concerning the Day of Pentecost.

"1 When the Day of Pentecost had fully come, they were all with one accord in one place. 2 And suddenly there came a sound from heaven, as of a rushing mighty wind, and it filled the whole house where they were sitting. 3 Then there appeared to them divided tongues, as of fire, and one sat upon each of them. 4 And they were all filled with the Holy Spirit and began to speak with other tongues, as the Spirit gave them utterance." **Acts 2:4**

In verses five through thirteen of the same chapter in Acts we learn the believers were filled with the Holy Spirit and spoke with other tongues. They were speaking in languages foreign to their understanding. They were speaking languages they had never learned. Paul wrote on this subject to the church at Corinth.

"13 Let him who speaks in a tongue pray that he may interpret. 14 For if I pray in a tongue, my spirit prays, but my understanding is unfruitful." **I Corinthians 14:13,14**

The tongues spoken by the believers on the Day of Pentecost were a sign and a wonder to the Jews who came to see the outpouring of the Holy Spirit. One hundred and twenty people were speaking in languages foreign to their understanding the wonderful works of God. How could the one hundred and twenty speak words they had never learned?

Acts 2:4 tells us plainly how they spoke words they had never learned. The one hundred and twenty *"began to speak with other tongues, as the Spirit gave them utterance"!* The Holy Spirit gave the believers utterance. Giving them utterance is the same thing as saying the Holy Spirit spoke to them. In order for the believers to speak with other tongues, they had to receive the utterance. Receiving utterance is the same thing as saying they heard the Holy Spirit's voice. When believers speak in tongues as the Spirit gives them utterance, they are hearing the voice of the Holy Spirit.

We must explore this truth applying what we have already learned and search for more to find all the understanding it contains. The natural man does not receive from the Holy Spirit. Believers receive utterance with their spirit. They hear the voice of the Holy Spirit with their inner man. The Holy Spirit does not speak to our natural ears nor to our intellect. He speaks to our spirit. We do not hear with the ears on the side of our head nor with the brains within our head, but rather with our spiritual ears in our inner man.

We need to understand where inside of us we receive utterance or hear the voice of the Holy Spirit. Our inner man has many parts.

> *"37 On the last day, that great day of the feast, Jesus stood and cried out, saying, "If anyone thirsts, let him come to Me and drink. 38 He who believes in Me, as the Scripture has said, out of his heart will flow rivers of living water." 39 But this He spoke concerning the Spirit, whom those believing in Him would receive; for the Holy Spirit was not yet given, because Jesus was not yet glorified."* **John 7:37-39**

Jesus said in verse thirty-eight *"out of the believers heart would flow rivers of living water"*. Strong's Exhaustive Concordance of the Bible lists the word translated **"...belly..."** in the King James version, (translated **"...heart..."** in the New King James version) as number **2836**. Strong's "Greek Dictionary of the New Testament" defines the Greek word listed number **2836**.

> **2836 koilia** from koilos ("hollow"); a cavity, i.e. (spec.) the abdomen; by impl. the matrix; fig. the heart: — belly, womb.

Jesus is not speaking figuratively in **John 7:38**, He is speaking plainly. He is telling us out of the area of the abdomen rivers of living water will flow. Every river has a place of beginning. The place of beginning of the river of living water which will flow out of the believer is the area of the abdomen.

Scripture also tells us in **John 7:39** the river of living water of which Jesus is speaking concerns *"the Spirit, whom* *those believing in Him would receive; for the Holy Spirit was not yet given, because Jesus was not yet glorified"*. The river of *"...living water..."* which will flow out of the believer comes from the Holy Spirit. The place of beginning of the Holy Spirit's ministry through the believer is within the believer from the area of the believer's abdomen.

We have seen again and again how Jesus uses natural illustrations to help us better understand spiritual matters. This illustration of a river flowing out of the believer is no exception. There are things Jesus wants us to understand about a natural river as we compare this natural thing to the ministry of the Holy Spirit as a spiritual thing.

A natural river flows through a certain channel. The channel is the course through which the water flows. Successful navigation down the river is determined by finding the channel of the river and maintaining direction within the channel. The water of the river, as a rule, always flows down the channel (exceptions do exist, such as flooding or drought).

The river of living water which flows out of the believer, flows through a certain channel. The beginning of the river is in the *"belly"*. The river flows from the belly out of the believer. The movement of this *"living water"* is through a certain channel from inner man, through natural man, out of the man. All water of the Holy Spirit which flows through the believer flows through this channel from within man. If you can find the channel, you can learn to successfully flow in the Spirit for all of His ministries to be fulfilled to you and through you.

FAITH TO SPEAK & HEAR

The kingdom of God operates *"...by grace through faith..."*. Beginning at new birth on into heaven itself, every step must be a step taken through faith. The Word says, *"...the just shall live by faith..."* **Romans 1:17** and *"...without faith it is impossible to please Him (God)..."* **Hebrews 11:6**. All of chapter two was devoted to God's will and faith. We learned God's will does not operate automatically, it is activated by faith. God's will concerning the ministries of neither the **Word** nor the **Spirit** operate automatically, it is activated by faith.

Chapter five examined the ministries of the Holy Spirit. We saw the Holy Spirit as advocate & comforter, teacher, supernatural memory, witness, guide, and convincer. In this chapter we are searching for understanding of how we receive ministry from the Holy Spirit. In the process of our search we learned one way the Holy Spirit ministers to us is by speaking to us. We saw the flow of living water from the Holy Spirit through us begins in our *"belly"*. We want to find the channel over which the water flows and learn to flow in it.

One of the simplest ways of finding the channel of the river which originates in our "belly" and flows through us is to consider a *"manifestation"* of the Holy Spirit. The Holy Spirit fulfills His ministry to us by manifesting Himself in many different ways. One of the manifestations of the Holy Spirit is tongues.

128

Acts 2:4 says the believers *"...were all filled with the Holy Spirit and began to speak with other tongues, as the Spirit gave them utterance"*. The utterance the believers received was a manifestation of the Holy Spirit. Many have misunderstood what the believers received on the Day of Pentecost. They think the believers received the "gift" of tongues. However, Jesus was very clear in the use of His words in what the believers were to receive.

> *"4 Being assembled together with them, He commanded them not to depart from Jerusalem, but to wait for the Promise of the Father, "which," He said, "you have heard from Me; 5 for John truly baptized with water, but you shall be baptized with the Holy Spirit not many days from now." 6 Therefore, when they had come together, they asked Him, saying, "Lord, will You at this time restore the kingdom to Israel?" 7 And He said to them, "It is not for you to know times or seasons which the Father has put in His own authority. 8 But you shall receive power when the Holy Spirit has come upon you; and you shall be witnesses to Me in Jerusalem, and in all Judea and Samaria, and to the end of the earth."*
>
> *Acts 1:4-8*

The promise of the Father was not power nor tongues, it was the Holy Spirit as we saw clearly in John chapters fourteen, fifteen, and sixteen. Power and tongues are simply two manifestations of the gift who is the Holy Spirit. Tongues divinely inspired by the Holy Spirit come to the believer as the Holy Spirit gives him utterance. This utterance begins as a response to the operation of faith.

Let us consider an easy to understand scriptural illustration of the operation of faith in doing the will of God before we consider tongues. Jesus ministered to a great multitude of people. The same evening He miraculously fed the multitude of five thousand men, besides women and children, with only five loaves and two fish. When they had all eaten and were full, the disciples took up twelve baskets full of fragments which remained. Jesus then gave His disciples instructions to cross the sea by boat.

> *"22 Immediately Jesus made His disciples get into the boat and go before Him to the other side, while He sent the multitudes away. 23 And when He had sent the multitudes away, He went up on the mountain by Himself to pray. Now when evening came, He was alone there. 24 But the boat was now in the middle of the sea, tossed by the waves, for the wind was contrary. 25 Now in the fourth watch of the night Jesus went to them, walking on the sea. 26 And when the disciples saw Him walking on the sea, they were troubled, saying, "It is a ghost!" And they cried out for fear. 27 But immediately Jesus spoke to them, saying, "Be of good cheer! It is I; do not be afraid." 28 And Peter answered Him and said, "Lord, if it is You, command me to come to You on the water." 29 So He said, "Come." And when Peter had come down out of the boat, he walked on the water to go to Jesus. 30 But when he saw that the wind was boisterous, he was afraid; and beginning to sink he cried out, saying, "Lord, save me!" 31 And immediately Jesus stretched out His hand and caught him, and said to him, "O you of little faith, why did you doubt?" 32 And when they got into the boat, the wind ceased. 33 Then those who were in the boat came and worshiped Him, saying, "Truly You are the Son of God."* **Matthew 14:22-33**

We will consider Peter walking on the water as our illustration of faith and the will of God. When Jesus commanded, *"Come"*, to Peter, He was speaking the will of God. Jesus made it clear He only came to do the will of His Father. Peter moved to the side of the boat to go out to Jesus in response to the will of God.

As a fisherman Peter knew it was impossible for a man to walk on water. He knew Jesus *"...walking on the sea..."* was a miracle. He also knew getting out of the boat and walking to Jesus was humanly impossible and required divine intervention. The miraculous power of God did not pick Peter up and set him out of the boat. Peter had to get *"down out of the boat"* in order to begin walking to Jesus. Peter knew he would have to walk by faith in order to do this.

There he is at the side of the boat looking down into the water of the sea. God did not raise a natural platform onto which Peter could step. *Matthew 14:29* says Peter *"walked on the water to go to Jesus"*. As Peter looked down, his natural eye could not see anything upon which to step but water. Because he knew water would not support a man, the only way he could step down out of the boat was by faith. That means he believed God would support him with His miraculous power if he would step out by faith to do what he was sure was the will of God.

Speaking in tongues operates the same way. The Holy Spirit does not give the utterance first but gives utterance only in response to faith. Faith comes first, not utterance. For Peter God did not provide a leg support first but supported his leg in response to Peter's faith. Scripture teaches *"...faith is the substance of things hoped for, the evidence of things not seen"* *Hebrews 11:1*. Faith comes first then the promise of God. We walk in faith in response to what we are sure is the will of God.

When a person speaks in tongues, he must first exercise faith in response to what he is sure is the will of God. He must *"step down out of the boat"* and *"walk on water with his tongue"*.

That means the person must begin speaking by faith first, and the Holy Spirit will support his tongue with divinely inspired utterance.

The response time between faith and utterance is not measured in natural time but rather in spiritual time. Even so, consider how rapidly response to stimuli can be in the natural. Consider touching a hot stove with the tip of your index finger. Many things happen the instant you touch the hot object. The nerve endings send a message through the hand, up the arm, into the brain saying there is a heat overload on the tip of the index finger. The brain, then, responds to the message by making a decision what to do in the matter. The brain sends the decision back down the arm, through the hand, into the finger for the finger to remove itself from the hot object. All of this only takes a split second. Think about the last time you touched a hot object how long it took you to remove your finger from the object.

Faster than the split second it takes for messages to be sent from finger to brain and back again, utterance is provided in response to faith. As long as faith is in operation, utterance will keep coming. The instant faith stops, utterance will stop. It was the same for Peter. When his natural sight, hearing, and understanding took over, his spiritual senses were short circuited and faith stopped. When his faith stopped, he began to sink beneath the waves.

> *"29 And when Peter had come down out of the boat, he walked on the water to go to Jesus. 30 But when he saw that the wind was boisterous, he was afraid; and beginning to sink he cried out, saying, "Lord, save me!"*

> *"31 And immediately Jesus stretched out His hand and caught him, and said to him, "O you of little faith, why did you doubt?"* **Matthew 14:29-31**

It was doubt and fear based on Peter seeing *"...the wind was boisterous..."* that made him stop walking in faith.

Often speaking in tongues is the same. I have seen it many times. A believer will exercise faith to speak in tongues, and the Holy Spirit responds by providing utterance. The believer hears the utterance coming out of his mouth and begins to doubt the sound he hears is really divinely inspired tongues. Doubt short circuits the believer's faith and utterance stops. Generally, a little reassurance from another believer that the utterance is really from the Holy Spirit is all the believer needs to begin speaking in tongues by faith again.

IDENTIFYING THE HOLY SPIRIT'S VOICE

Understanding the process of speaking in tongues is very helpful for learning to identify and develop the channel of communication between the Holy Spirit and the believer. It is important to know that faith comes first and, then, the Holy Spirit responds to your faith by providing divinely inspired utterance. You do not receive the utterance first and then speak but rather exercise faith first and then receive the utterance. Receiving utterance from the Holy Spirit is the same thing as hearing the voice of the Holy Spirit. Every time the believer speaks in tongues divinely inspired by the Holy Spirit, he is hearing the voice of the Holy Spirit.

The more you pray in tongues with this understanding, the easier it will be for you to learn to identify the voice of the Holy Spirit. It will also be easier to learn to identify the channel through which the water flows from your belly up and out of your mouth. Through this same channel the river of living water for all of the Holy Spirit's ministries flow within the believer. Ask the Holy Spirit to identify His voice for you. Think while you are speaking in tongues, "The Holy Spirit is giving me utterance for me to be able to speak in tongues. I am receiving the utterance He is giving me. Receiving utterance is the same thing as hearing His voice. I am hearing the voice of the Holy Spirit. What does His voice sound like to my spirit? How does it flow through me as I speak?" Continued "listening" and "thinking" while speaking in tongues will help identify the voice of the Holy Spirit and the channel through which it flows.

I was in India several years ago conducting seminars for ministers. At the end of several weeks I was in the departure lounge ready to clear passport control for my return journey to the U.S.A.. There were many people in the line both ahead of me and behind me. As time passed the two persons behind me began talking rather loudly in a language that sounded different than what I had been hearing in India the past several weeks although there was a familiar sound to it. Soon I was certain I knew what language they were speaking and the nation in which it was spoken. I turned around and said, "You are speaking Ibo from Nigeria, aren't you"? The two people laughed and said, "Yes! How did you know"? I told them I had spent several weeks among the Ibo people in Nigeria only a short time before this India trip and had grown accustomed to the sound of the language.

The more you hear the voice of a person or the language of a people the easier it is to identify the person or the language group. When I call home from the road, I never identify myself to my three children nor to my wife of forty-four years. Nor do they have to tell me their names. We are so familiar with the sound of each others' voices, we easily identify one another.

In Thailand many years ago conducting a seminar for ministers and church leaders right in the middle of a teaching session, the Holy Spirit began to speak to my spirit about one of the participants. The Holy Spirit pointed out a man and told me certain things about him. He told me to go to the man and say certain things to him. In the spirit I said I would just as soon as I completed the teaching session. The Holy Spirit told me to go right then. So I stopped right in the middle of the session, walked over to the man, and began to speak to him the words the Holy Spirit had given me for him. The man received the ministry, repented for the actions the Holy Spirit had revealed to me in which he had been involved, and instantly received the Holy Spirit and began speaking in tongues!

The more we speak in other tongues divinely inspired by the Holy Spirit the more familiar we will become with the sound of His voice and the flow of it through our spirit. Then when He speaks to us in our mother tongue, words easy to be understood, we will know it is the same voice we have heard so often in the familiar setting of tongues. The Holy Spirit only has one voice. Whether He is giving us utterance in a tongue foreign to our understanding or utterance easy to be understood, He uses the only voice He has to do both. Whether you speak a foreign language or your mother tongue, you must use the only voice you have to speak both. Whenever the Holy Spirit ministers to us, comforting, teaching, bringing to our remembrance, testifying, guiding, or convincing us, we will recognize His voice. Properly identifying and becoming familiar with His voice is essential for successfully receiving ministry from Him when He ministers to us by speaking to us!

Chapter Seven

MANIFESTATION OF THE SPIRIT

Paul wrote of the *"manifestation"* of the Spirit in his letter to the church at Corinth.

> *"4 There are diversities of gifts, but the same Spirit. 5 There are differences of ministries, but the same Lord. 6 And there are diversities of activities, but it is the same God who works all in all. 7 But the manifestation of the Spirit is given to each one for the profit of all."*
>
> *I Corinthians 12:4-7*

Strong's Exhaustive Concordance of the Bible lists the word *"manifestation"* as number **5321**. Strong's "Greek Dictionary of the New Testament" defines the Greek word listed as number **5321**.

> **5321** *phanerosis* from 5319; exhibition, i.e. (Fig.) expression, (by extens.) a bestowment: -- manifestation.

Webster's New Universal Unabridged Dictionary defines **manifestation** and **manifest**.

> **manifestation** - 1. a manifesting or being manifested. 2. something that manifests. 3. a public demonstration, as by a government, party, etc., for political effect.

manifest - plain; open; clearly visible to the eye or obvious to the understanding; apparent; not obscure or difficult to be seen or understood.

1. to make clear or evident; to show plainly; reveal.
2. to prove; to be evidence of; to appear to the senses; to show itself.

Paul uses the same Greek word in his second letter to the church at Corinth in a completely different context unrelated to the Holy Spirit. To look at the usage in this second context will help us understand the meaning of the word in relation to the Holy Spirit.

> *"2 We have renounced the hidden things of shame, not walking in craftiness nor handling the word of God deceitfully, but by manifestation of the truth commending ourselves to every man's conscience in the sight of God."*
> ***II Corinthians 4:2***

From definition and usage we can see manifestation means revealed, not hidden. When this term is used as a manifestation of the Spirit, then, it means the Holy Spirit reveals an aspect of Himself and of His ability to us. Paul wrote, *"the manifestation of the Spirit is given to each one for the profit of all"*. King James version of the Bible says, *"the manifestation of the Spirit is given to every man to profit withal"*. In other words, the Holy Spirit is willing to provide revelation of Himself and of His ability to help us profit. We have already seen the Holy Spirit has been sent by the Father at the request of Jesus on our behalf. ***The Holy Spirit is coming to help us!***

In order to fulfill His ministries of advocate/comforter, teacher, supernatural memory, witness, guide, and convincer, He must manifest or reveal Himself and His ability to us. The Triune God is infinite without beginning or ending. Revelation of any one of the three parts of the Trinity would be endless. It would be impossible to exhaust all of the revelation of God. The Holy Spirit is willing to reveal Himself and His ability to us any way necessary, from an infinite array of possibilities, according to the will of God to help us.

He will manifest Himself and His ability in more ways than just to comfort, teach, bring to our remembrance, testify, guide, or convince us. When the Holy Spirit gives utterance to believers for them to speak in tongues, He is providing revelation of His ability to the believer. That makes tongues a manifestation of the Spirit. We are going to consider tongues as a manifestation of the Spirit.

TONGUES

At the beginning of the Church the New Testament records tremendous controversy surrounding the issue of circumcision. The issue was only able to be resolved by accurately dividing the Word and by receiving divine input from the Holy Spirit. The letter of resolution sent by the apostles and elders from the church at Jerusalem to the Gentile believers abroad contained a wonderful statement. It said, *"It seemed good to the Holy Spirit, and to us..." **Acts 15:28**.* Resolution to all controversy and conflict within the Church should contain the same statement, *"It seems good to the Holy Spirit, and to us..."*

Tongues has been a modern day "issue of circumcision" within the Church. Much division has come from lack of knowledge and understanding of tongues. Remember the Word of the Lord prophesied through the prophet Hosea, *"My people are destroyed for lack of knowledge"* **Hosea 4:6**. Just like circumcision, the controversy of tongues can only be resolved by accurately dividing the Word and by receiving divine input from the Holy Spirit. With these two things working, and an open heart to hear what the Spirit is saying, controversy can be removed from tongues. Then the Church can walk united in the matter.

Most Christians who receive the Bible as the inspired Word of God accept that one hundred and twenty believers spoke *"with other tongues, as the Spirit gave them utterance"* on the Day of Pentecost. Many accept that believers can *"speak with other tongues, as the Spirit gives them utterance"* today. The main areas of controversy which divide believers seem to be who can speak in tongues, what is the purpose of tongues, and when can tongues be spoken. If we could help bring simple scriptural based knowledge and understanding in these areas, it would help remove fear, doubt, controversy, and division.

WHO CAN SPEAK IN TONGUES

The most crucial element to understanding this matter we have already considered. Tongues is not the gift the believers receive. Let us look at two scripture references regarding the gift the believers are to receive. Jesus Himself is speaking intimately with His disciples in both illustrations.

"15 If you love Me, keep My commandments. 16 And I will pray the Father, and He will give you another Helper, that He may abide with you forever. 17 the Spirit of truth, whom the world cannot receive, because it neither sees Him nor knows Him; but you know Him, for He dwells with you and will be in you." **John 14:15-17**

In verse sixteen above Jesus says He *"will pray the Father, and He will give you another Helper"*. When one person gives another person something, the thing given is called a *"gift"*. The Father is giving the disciples another Helper. **John 14:26** says, *"the Helper, the Holy Spirit, whom the Father will send in My name"*. **The gift the Father is giving the disciples is the Holy Spirit** *"that He may abide with you forever"*.

"9 So I say to you, ask, and it will be given to you; seek, and you will find; knock, and it will be opened to you. 10 For everyone who asks receives, and he who seeks finds, and to him who knocks it will be opened. 11 If a son asks for bread from any father among you, will he give him a stone? Or if he asks for a fish, will he give him a serpent instead of a fish? 12 Or if he asks for an egg, will he offer him a scorpion? 13 If you then, being evil, know how to give good gifts to your children, how much more will your heavenly Father give the Holy Spirit to those who ask Him!" **Luke 11:9-13**

Jesus is speaking about giving and receiving. He says *"If you then, being evil, know how to give good gifts to your children..."*. Comparing natural fathers with our heavenly Father, Jesus then says *"...how much more will your heavenly Father give the Holy Spirit to those who ask Him!"*. Jesus has made a direct comparison between the *"...good gifts..."* natural fathers give and *"...the Holy Spirit..."* given by heavenly Father. **The Holy Spirit is the gift the believers receive.**

Partial answer to our question, "Who can speak in tongues?", is very simple and direct. Only those who are born again are candidates to speak in tongues inspired by the Holy Spirit. Jesus has already told us *"...the Spirit of truth, whom the world cannot receive, because it neither sees Him nor knows Him..." John 14:17*. Tongues is a manifestation of the Holy Spirit and the world cannot receive the Holy Spirit. Therefore, the world cannot speak in tongues as a manifestation from the Holy Spirit.

There are three sources of tongues; the Holy Spirit, demonic spirits, and humans. The world may speak in tongues inspired by demonic spirits or their own selves but not inspired by the Holy Spirit. Believers could receive inspiration from a demonic spirit or speak in tongues from their own selves if their hearts are not turned toward the Lord and they are not walking with God. However, if believers desire to receive utterance exclusively from the Holy Spirit, Jesus' Word recorded in *Luke 11:9-13* serves as a guarantee of protection against our receiving tongues of darkness from a demonic spirit. He told us natural fathers would not give their children stones for bread, serpents for fish, or scorpions for eggs. He then compared natural fathers with our heavenly Father. *"If you then, being evil, know how to give good gifts to your children, how much more will your heavenly Father give the Holy Spirit to those who ask Him!"*

Consider your own natural lives. In your childhood how much time did you spend worrying your natural father was going to give you a stone, a serpent, or a scorpion if you asked him for bread, fish, or an egg? If you have children, how much time do your children spend worrying over the same thing; or how much time do you waste considering whether or not you are going to give your children stones, serpents, or scorpions when they ask you for bread, fish, or eggs? As a rule children feel protection and confidence in their parents' home when they are in need. If we as natural parents can create an atmosphere of confidence and protection for our children, how much more can our heavenly Father if we will only trust Him!

We have seen the Holy Spirit manifesting Himself or revealing Himself to give the believers utterance for them to speak in tongues in *Acts 2:4*. In order to answer our question, "Who can speak in tongues?", more thoroughly we must find the purpose of tongues. We will temporarily leave considering who can speak in tongues to consider the purpose of tongues.

WHAT IS THE PURPOSE OF TONGUES...

Paul devoted considerable time to the purpose of tongues in his first letter to the church at Corinth. We will use the fourteenth chapter as our primary reference. Within this portion of scripture Paul focuses on the corporate gathering of the church. The general purpose of the entire letter was to deal with problems in the church; problems of strife, division, and lack of order. Paul deals with tongues in relation to corporate problems when the church assembles together. However, what he was inspired to write about the use of tongues corporately is also relevant to the individual believer in his private life.

> *"2 He who speaks in a tongue does not speak to men but to God, for no one understands him; however, in the spirit he speaks mysteries."*

> *"4 He who speaks in a tongue edifies himself, but he who prophesies edifies the church."*

> *"14 If I pray in a tongue, my spirit prays, but my understanding is unfruitful."*

"15 What is the conclusion then? I will pray with the spirit, and I will also pray with the understanding. I will sing with the spirit, and I will sing with the understanding."

"39 Therefore, brethren, desire earnestly to prophesy, and do not forbid to speak with tongues."

There is a wealth of knowledge deposited in these few verses of scripture. We will search for understanding, with help from the Holy Spirit, for all of it.

Verse fourteen tells us when I pray in a tongue *"my spirit prays"*. This is easy to understand if we remember what Paul wrote in *I Corinthians 2:9-14*. *"The natural man does not receive the things of the Spirit of God, for they are foolishness to him; nor can he know them, because they are spiritually discerned."* The Holy Spirit gives believers the utterance to speak in tongues. Those speaking receive the utterance with their spirit. It is their spirit who prays the utterance they have received. Our soul and body are involved only as necessary parts for us to speak out of our mouths.

Jesus expects us to grow in our understanding of spiritual matters. He wants us to come to understand the difference between our natural parts and our spiritual parts. When He ministered to Nicodemus about the difference between natural and spiritual, Nicodemus did not understand. Jesus' response was rather sharp to Nicodemus because he was a teacher of Israel.

"10 Jesus answered and said to him, "Are you the teacher of Israel, and do not know these things? 11 Most assuredly, I say to you, We speak what We know and testify what We have seen, and you do not receive Our witness. 12 If I have told you earthly things and you do not believe, how will you believe if I tell you heavenly things?" **John 3:10-12**

Unless we gain a working understanding of our spirit, the spiritual world, and the Holy Spirit, how could we ever *"...walk in the spirit and you shall not fulfill the lust of the flesh..."?*

Verse fourteen also tells us *"my spirit prays, but my understanding is unfruitful"*. The contrast here is between understanding and not understanding. This is not a contrast between natural and spiritual. The Holy Spirit will manifest Himself for us to have understanding in our spirit. However, tongues is not a manifestation of the Holy Spirit we understand in our spirit. The contrast is between understanding in our spirit versus not understanding in our spirit.

Verse two tells us *"he who speaks in a tongue does not speak to men but to God, for no one understands him; however, in the spirit he speaks mysteries"*. The Father has decided the utterance the Holy Spirit gives us will be a mystery. He has also decided the utterance will not be spoken to men but directly to God.

At this time I do not have revelation why God has decided these things, but we can be confident in at least two things in the matter: God knows best, and He wants the best for us. His decision to keep the utterance mysterious from our understanding was a divine decision for our good.

> *"11 For I know the thoughts that I think toward you, says the Lord, thoughts of peace and not of evil, to give you a future and a hope."* **Jeremiah 29:11**

> *"17 Every good gift and every perfect gift is from above, and comes down from the Father of lights, with whom there is no variation or shadow of turning."* **James 1:17**

In teaching on the person and ministry of the Holy Spirit so many times I have had believers ask, "If I cannot understand what I am speaking or praying, then, what good is it and why should I do it?" Even if the only answer we had was tongues is a manifestation of God the Holy Spirit, that should be enough to make us desire to have it. Divine utterance flowing through us by inspiration of the Holy Spirit, whether mysterious to our understanding or not, is the will of the Father. Jesus has made it perfectly clear the Father is sending the Holy Spirit as our Helper. Whatever the Father wills for the Holy Spirit to do in relation to us as believers will be to help us have life!

...for EDIFICATION

Verse four tells us *"he who speaks in a tongue edifies himself"*. Strong's Exhaustive Concordance of the Bible lists the word *"...edifies..."* as number **3618**. Strong's "Greek Dictionary of the New Testament" defines the Greek word listed as number **3618**.

> **3618** *oikodomeo* from the same as 3619; to be a householder, i.e. construct or (fig.) confirm: -- (be in) build (-er, -ing, up), edify, embolden.

Webster's New Universal Unabridged Dictionary defines **edify**.

> **edify** - 1. to build; to establish. 2. to instruct and improve the mind of, particularly morally or spiritually. to be improved or enlightened.

Manifestation

The main components of meaning of the word deal with building up, improving, or establishing. That means the person speaking in a tongue is being built up, improved, or established in the spirit. This building up of the believer's spirit helps the believer move in the spirit as God designed us to move.

Verse four says *"he who speaks in a tongue edifies himself"*. It is the flow of divinely inspired utterance from the Holy Spirit that is edifying the believer. The believer is edifying himself only in the sense that he is the one doing the speaking as the Holy Spirit gives him utterance.

A natural illustration will help our understanding. A car battery contains electrical current stored inside the battery. The power contained in the battery helps start the engine of the car for the car to move as designed. Under certain conditions the electrical current can be discharged leaving the battery in low supply of current. If the discharge of electrical current is great enough, the battery cannot start the engine. The battery must then be connected to a power source for recharging. When the battery is connected to the power source and the power source activated, the battery can be recharged. Depending on the rate of discharge it can take from only a few minutes to a full day to recharge the battery back to normal operating levels. Only with a charged up battery can the engine be started to make the car move as designed.

Let us consider another writer's understanding of this very same aspect of tongues. Jude, a servant of Jesus Christ, and brother of James wrote to believers regarding being built up by praying in tongues.

"20 But you, beloved, building yourselves up on your most holy faith, praying in the Holy Spirit." **Jude 20**

Knowledge and understanding we have gained from *I Corinthians* chapter fourteen regarding tongues and their purpose are as follows:

1. When a believer prays or speaks in tongues by in-spiration of the Holy Spirit, his spirit is praying or speaking.

2. The utterance the believer receives from the Holy Spirit while speaking in tongues is mysterious to his understanding.

3. The utterance, which is a mystery, is not spoken to man but directly to God.

4. The decision for the utterance to remain a mystery to the believer was made by God.

5. The Lord our God knows best and wants the best for us. His decision was for our good.

6. The divine utterance flowing through us by inspira-tion of the Holy Spirit is according to the will of the Father for the Holy Spirit to help us.

7. The believer speaking in tongues is being edified, built up in spirit, by the divine flow of utterance while he is speaking in tongues.

Manifestation

...for PRAYER

We must consider another purpose of tongues. The Holy Spirit inspired Paul to write, *"if I pray in a tongue, my spirit prays, but my understanding is unfruitful"* **I Corinthians 14:14**. When a believer speaks in tongues, he is edified from the flow of the divinely inspired utterance. However, the utterance is more than just edification for the individual believer. The utterance is also a divinely inspired *"...prayer..."*. When the believer speaks in tongues inspired by the Holy Spirit, his spirit is actually praying.

Jesus made it clear the Holy Spirit has been sent to help us as believers. We have begun to see diversities of ways the Holy Spirit may fulfill His ministry to help us. Paul wrote to the church at Rome regarding one of the ways the Holy Spirit helps us.

> *"26 Likewise the Spirit also helps in our weaknesses. For we do not know what we should pray for as we ought, but the Spirit Himself makes intercession for us with groanings which cannot be uttered."* **Romans 8:26**

In this verse of scripture we see the Holy Spirit helps us as He Himself makes intercession for us. His prayers are with *"groanings which cannot be uttered"*. However, the Holy Spirit will provide us with help in the form of tongues which can be uttered. Paul wrote, *"What is the conclusion then? I will pray with the spirit, and I will also pray with the understanding"* **I Corinthians 14:15**. There are times when we will pray with our understanding but there are also times when we will pray with tongues foreign to our understanding. The Holy

Spirit can and will provide us with the utterance to pray in both tongues foreign to our understanding and utterance we understand.

We may ask for this utterance under at least two conditions: 1) when we know we should pray, but we do not know for what we should pray, and 2) when we know for what we are praying, but we are not sure how to pray. We can pray in tongues in both instances with confidence the Holy Spirit will inspire a perfect prayer!

...for PRAISE & WORSHIP

Another form of help the Holy Spirit provides through tongues is in worship. Jesus spoke of one of the ministries of the Holy Spirit. *"He will glorify Me, for He will take of what is Mine and declare it to you" **John 16:13***. We see this demonstrated on the Day of Pentecost when the believers were speaking in tongues for the first time. The devout Jews who came to see the outpouring of the Holy Spirit said, *"...we hear them speaking in our own tongues the wonderful works of God..." **Acts 2:11***.

Paul wrote, *"I will sing with the spirit, and I will also sing with the understanding" **I Corinthians 14:15***. When the believer is worshipping God, he may call on the Holy Spirit for utterance to worship in tongues. This is another form of help the Holy Spirit provides the believer.

We have seen tongues does not just have one purpose. Now that we have gained certain knowledge and understanding regarding some of the purposes of tongues we can return to our search to find out who can speak in tongues.

WHO CAN SPEAK IN TONGUES

Our partial answer to the question, "Who can speak in tongues?", stated only those born again are candidates to speak in tongues inspired by the Holy Spirit. In order to answer the question more specifically we will ask the question more specifically. We will use our partial answer and the knowledge acquired regarding some of the purposes of tongues to help us form a more specific question.

"Which of the Father's children does He desire to have the Holy Spirit help by giving them a flow of divine utterance to edify, build them up in spirit, help them pray a perfect prayer, or worship the Lord?"

The answer is all of the Father's children! Our Father desires for the Holy Spirit to help every child of His be edified, built up in spirit, to pray, and to worship the Lord. While there are many ways in God of being built up in spirit, one way is speaking in tongues. While prayer has many forms, tongues is one form. And while worship, too, has many forms, tongues is one form.

God has not given tongues as a cure-all solution to growth in the spirit. Nor has He meant for tongues to be the primary way of edification. Certainly tongues is not the only form of prayer or worship. However, to ignore tongues as one way to be edified, to pray, or to worship would be wrong.

Tongues are simple, easy to speak, easy to identify as from the Holy Spirit, mysteries spoken directly to God unable to be hindered by anyone, divinely inspired unable to be tarnished by doubt or unbelief, an instant flow of the Spirit to edify the speaker, and the will of God. There is only one problem! Tongues will not operate automatically. They must be spoken by faith. The Holy Spirit will not speak in tongues for you. He will give you the utterance in response to your faith but you must exercise faith first to speak in tongues. Many believers are so full of fear and doubt concerning tongues they will not *"...get out of the boat..."*. **However, if we will open our hearts to our heavenly Father and to the Holy Spirit we can add a new dimension to our spiritual lives. We can learn to flow in the Spirit!**

WHEN CAN TONGUES BE SPOKEN

In this section of the book we are considering tongues as a manifestation of the Spirit in the private lives of individual believers for their personal edification, for help in prayer, and worship. We will ask the question, "When can tongues be spoken?", as it applies to personal edification, prayer, and worship.

When can tongues be spoken for the individual's personal edification? There are three things we have learned about tongues spoken to edify the believer which will shape our understanding here.

1. Tongues are mysteries.

2. Tongues are spoken to God not to men.

3. Tongues are foreign to our understanding.

Because of these three facts, tongues spoken for the individual believer's personal edification should be done in private. However, they may be spoken as often as the believer desires or needs.

> *"18 I thank my God I speak with tongues more than you all; 19 yet in the church I would rather speak five words with my understanding, that I may teach others also, than ten thousand words in a tongue."* **I Corinthians 14:18,19**

When can tongues be spoken for the individual to pray divinely inspired by the Holy Spirit? There is a broader arena for this aspect of tongues than for personal edification. If the believer is praying about a personal matter this should be done in private. However, there are many times we may come together corporately to pray about a matter. Peter's imprisonment was such a case.

> *"1 Now about that time Herod the king stretched out his hand to harass some from the church. 2 Then he killed James the brother of John with the sword. 3 And because he saw that it pleased the Jews, he proceeded further to seize Peter also. Now it was during the Days of Unleavened Bread. 4 So when he had arrested him, he put him in prison, and delivered him to four squads of soldiers to keep him, intending to bring him before the people after Passover. 5 Peter was therefore kept in prison, but constant prayer was offered to God for him by the church. ...12 So, when he (Peter) had considered this, he came to the house of Mary, the mother of John whose surname was Mark, where many were gathered together praying."*
> *Acts 12:1-5,12*

If we are gathered together as believers for the purpose of praying about a matter, we may call on the Holy Spirit to give us utterance to help us pray. Amos the prophet asked, *"Can two walk together, except they be agreed?"* **Amos 3:3**. The first priority in this situation is to determine the level of knowledge and understanding of the believers involved in prayer regarding tongues and the Holy Spirit. If they understand this purpose of tongues and the ministry of the Holy Spirit to help us pray, it will be easy for all to be in agreement to call on the Holy Spirit for utterance to pray in tongues.

When can tongues be spoken or sung for the individual to worship God? This area, too, like prayer in tongues, is broader than tongues for personal edification. Any time in private worship the individual can call on the Holy Spirit for utterance to praise, worship, and glorify the Lord. It is also possible when the church is assembled and worshipping the Lord for tongues to be spoken or sung. This aspect of tongues must operate on the principle of agreement in order to avoid strife and confusion. The congregation must be in agreement to allow tongues to flow as an expression of praise and worship. There is hardly a sound in heaven or on earth as pure and awesome as a congregation singing together in tongues. Divinely inspired utterance flowing through believers glorifying their Lord!

Chapter Eight
THE ANOINTING OF GOD

At the beginning of Jesus' ministry He went up to Nazareth and entered the synagogue on the Sabbath day. It was His intention to read a portion of scripture and give the people certain revelation about Himself.

> *"17 And He was handed the book of the prophet Isaiah. And when He had opened the book, He found the place where it was written: 18 "The Spirit of the Lord is upon Me, because He has anointed Me to preach the gospel to the poor; He has sent Me to heal the brokenhearted, to proclaim liberty to the captives and recovery of sight to the blind, to set at liberty those who are oppressed; 19 to proclaim the acceptable year of the Lord." 20 Then He closed the book, and gave it back to the attendant and sat down. And the eyes of all who were in the synagogue were fixed on Him. 21 And He began to say to them, "Today this Scripture is fulfilled in your hearing."*
>
> ***Luke 4:17-21***

When Jesus spoke the words, *"Today this Scripture is fulfilled in your hearing"*, He was revealing to the people that He was the person about whom Isaiah was prophesying in this scripture. He was telling the people that He was fulfillment of the prophecy.

In other words, Jesus was telling the people the Spirit of the Lord was upon Him because He had been anointed to do certain things. In the spirit there is an inseparable connection between the Holy Spirit and the anointing. If we are going to learn about the Holy Spirit and to flow in the spirit then we must also learn about the anointing.

In order to learn more about the anointing let us consider the Spirit of the Lord and the anointing in Jesus' life. In Chapter One we carefully considered Jesus' walk on the earth as a man, laying aside His own attributes as God. In Luke chapter four Jesus told us *"The Spirit of the Lord is upon Me because He has anointed Me to...*

...preach the gospel to the poor;

...heal the broken hearted,

...to proclaim liberty to the captives and...

...recovery of sight to the blind,

...to set at liberty those who are oppressed;

...to proclaim the acceptable year of the Lord."

These six statements of ministry combined together make up the entire earthly ministry of Jesus, either directly or indirectly. We could say, then, the Spirit of the Lord and the anointing in Jesus' life are what caused Him to be able to fulfill His ministry on the earth!

IDENTIFYING THE ANOINTING

We need a clearer look at the anointing, a scriptural base upon which we can support our understanding. John's first epistle provides us with the beginning of just such a base. John is writing to the church about their state of growth in the spirit. He is emphasizing their need to fellowship with one another in the light as a result of having first walked in the light. He is writing these things as a warning so they will not be caught up in the world and the darkness in it. He writes of deceptions of the enemy desiring to pull them away from the truth.

> *"18 Little children, it is the last hour; and as you have heard that the Antichrist is coming, even now many antichrists have come, by which we know that it is the last hour. 19 They went out from us, but they were not of us; for if they had been of us, they would have continued with us; but they went out that they might be made manifest, that none of them were of us. 20 But you have an anointing from the Holy One, and you know all things. 21 I have not written to you because you do not know the truth, but because you know it, and that no lie is of the truth. 22 Who is a liar but he who denies that Jesus is the Christ? He is antichrist who denies the Father and the Son. 23 Whoever denies the Son does not have the Father either; he who acknowledges the Son has the Father also. 24 Therefore let that abide in you which you heard from the beginning. If what you heard from the beginning abides in you, you also will abide in the Son and in the Father. 25 And this is the promise that He has promised us eternal life. 26 these things I have written to you concerning those who try to deceive you. 27 But the anointing which you have received from Him abides in you, and you do not need that anyone teach you; but as the same anointing teaches you concerning all things, and is true, and is not a lie, and just as it has taught you, you will abide in Him." I John 2:18-27*

Notice verses twenty and twenty-seven very carefully. John writes of the *"...anointing..."* in both verses. He reveals four things in these two verses which will help guide us into greater understanding concerning the anointing.

...the anointing...you have received from Him (God)...

...the anointing...abides in you...

...the anointing...is true...

...the anointing...teaches you concerning all things...

These four things serve as a type of fingerprint for the anointing. There are identifying characteristics concerning certain things and beings which make them unmistakable. For example, one who came from heaven to live on earth as a human being, born of a virgin, lived sinless, died as the Lamb of God to take away the sin of the world, and rose again on the third day after crucifixion. That "fingerprint" can only identify Jesus.

The four characteristics of which John writes in *I John 2:20,27* are unmistakable identification. They identify the *anointing*. If we looked in the gospel written by John, we would find a match of these same four identifying characteristics. The gospel written by John uses a different name instead of the *anointing* as the one identified by these characteristics.

We have spent a great deal of time and detail considering the fourteenth, fifteenth, and sixteenth chapters in the gospel written by John. In them we have gained considerable knowledge and understanding about the person and ministry of the Holy Spirit. Four things we learned are...

...the heavenly Father will give believers another Helper...

...that He may abide with you forever...and will be in you...

...the Helper is the Spirit of truth...

...the Spirit of truth will guide you into all truth...

These four things match what we have learned from *I John* concerning the anointing. As we have already stated, there are identifying characteristics concerning certain things or beings which make them unmistakable. The four identifying characteristics from *I John* and from the gospel of *John* serve as a "fingerprint" identifying only one thing or being.

In the gospel of *John* Jesus said these four characteristics identify the Holy Spirit whom He also called the Helper and the Spirit of truth. In *I John* John said these four characteristics identify the Anointing. Whether we use the name Holy Spirit, Helper, Spirit of truth, or Anointing, the four identifying characteristics are the same. He is a gift from the heavenly Father, abides in the believers, is truth, and guides believers into all truth. That means the Anointing about whom John wrote in his first epistle and the Holy Spirit are one in the same. The Anointing is not a thing but a being. The Anointing is the Holy Spirit. **The Holy Spirit is the Anointing of God!**

An Expository Dictionary of New Testament Words by W.E. Vine defines the Greek word **"...*chrisma*..."** translated as **"...*anointing*..."** in English.

Chrisma - signifies an unguent, or an anointing. It was prepared from oil and aromatic herbs. It is used only metaphorically in the N.T.; by metonymy, of the Holy Spirit, I John 2:20,27, twice. The R.V. translates it *"anointing"* in all three places, instead of the A.V. *"unction"* and *"anointing"*.

That believers have *"an anointing from the Holy One"* indicates that this anointing renders them holy, separating them to God. The passage teaches that the gift of the Holy Spirit is the all-efficient means of enabling believers to possess a knowledge of the truth.

Notice he says *"...chrisma..."* is used *"...by metonymy, of the Holy Spirit, I John 2:20,27, twice..."*. In order to understand what he means here, we must learn what the word *"...metonymy..."* means. Websters New Universal Unabridged Dictionary defines **metonymy**.

metonymy - a change of name; use of the name of one thing for that of another associated with or suggested by it (e.g., "the White House has decided" for "the President has decided").

That means the term *"...chrisma..."* is used as a name for the Spirit of God instead of using the terms *"...Holy Spirit..."* as the name for the Spirit of God in *I John 2:20,27*. This supports what we have already discovered from the four identifying characteristics serving as a fingerprint for the Holy Spirit and the Anointing.

Each name Jesus used referring to the Spirit of God added some new dimension of understanding to help us better relate to Him. For example, when Jesus initially began to introduce the Holy Spirit, He told His disciples He would ask the Father to send them another Helper because He was going away from them. By using the name Helper Jesus was establishing the basis by which the disciples could relate to the Holy Spirit. If the Holy Spirit is also called the Helper, then the disciples could expect the Holy Spirit to help them.

SPECIAL ENDOWMENT

Now we see the Holy Spirit is also called the Anointing. We must find out exactly what this reveals about the Holy Spirit and what it establishes for our relationship with Him. The first place we will look is at the word *"...Anointing..."* used as a name for the Holy Spirit.

Strong's Exhaustive Concordance of the Bible lists the English word translated *"...anointing..."* in *I John 2:20,27* as number **5545**. Strong's "Greek Dictionary of the New Testament" defines the Greek word listed as number 5545.

> **5545** *chrisma* from 5548; an unguent or smearing, i.e. (fig.) the spec. endowment ("chrism") of the Holy Spirit: -- anointing, unction.

From this definition we see unguent or smearing does not directly apply. Even though the Holy Spirit is symbolically referred to as *"...oil..."* He is not literally an unguent or smearing just as He was not literally a *"...dove..."* when descending upon Jesus. Instead we must look at the figurative sense of the term, "...the special endowment ("chrism") of the Holy Spirit...".

Helper as a name for the Spirit of God reveals what we can expect to receive from Him: Help. Holy Spirit as a name for the Spirit of God reveals the Spirit's holy attribute or character. Spirit of truth as a name for the Spirit of God reveals the Spirit's inability to lie or be associated with lies but is truth. This John confirmed in *I John 2:27* when he said the Anointing, *"...is true, and is not a lie...".* Anointing as a name for the Spirit of God reveals the special endowment of the Holy Spirit to us.

What is an endowment? Webster's New Universal Unabridged Dictionary defines **endowment**.

> **endowment** - 1. an endowing. 2. that with which something is endowed; bequest; gift. 3. that which is given or bestowed on the person or mind; gift of nature; talent; ability.
>
> Synonyms - gift, provision, benefit, benefaction, capacity, attainment, qualification.

The special endowment of the Holy Spirit to us would be, then, the ability, provision, capacity, or qualification with which He provides us.

PURPOSE FOR THE ANOINTING

The next question we must ask is, "What is the purpose of this special endowment?" Another way of asking the same thing would be, "What is the purpose of the Anointing?" For what purpose does the Holy Spirit provide us ability, provision, capacity, or qualification? We will start with John's use of the term *"...anointing..."* in his first epistle, *I John 2:18-27*.

John wrote specifically regarding the purpose of the anointing in verses twenty and twenty seven.

> *"20 But you have an anointing from the Holy One, and you know all things... 27 But the anointing which you have received from Him abides in you, and you do not need that anyone teach you; but as the same anointing teaches you concerning all things, and it true, and is not a lie, and just as it has taught you, you will abide in Him."*

John said *"...you know all things..."* and *"...the anointing teaches you concerning all things...".* The context in which these words were written was very specific regarding the purpose of the Anointing. The knowledge and teaching the believers had received and would receive from the Anointing was...

1. ...to cause them to know the truth so they could abide successfully in Jesus as the Truth and the Father, and...

2. ...out of their knowledge of the truth they could be kept from the lies and deceptions of the enemy.

The top priority of the Spirit of God as the Anointing is to provide us with the ability to know Jesus and the Father. **It is only through the Anointing, the special endowment of the Holy Spirit, that we can know God!**

We stated earlier in this chapter "the Spirit of the Lord and the anointing in Jesus' life are what caused Him to be able to fulfill His ministry on the earth!" Now that we understand the Spirit of the Lord and the Anointing are one in the same, we can simplify this statement about Jesus' life and ministry. The Holy Spirit as the Anointing in Jesus' life is what caused Him to be able to fulfill His ministry on the earth.

Let us examine a scriptural illustration of Jesus fulfilling one aspect of His ministry on earth by the Anointing.

> *"22   Then one was brought to Him who was demon-possessed, blind and mute; and He healed him, so that the blind and mute man both spoke and saw. 23 And all the multitudes were amazed and said, "Could this be the Son of David?" 24 Now when the Pharisees heard it they said, "This fellow does not cast out demons except by Beelzebub, the ruler of the demons." 25 But Jesus knew their thoughts, and said to them: "Every kingdom divided against itself is brought to desolation, and every city or house divided against itself will not stand. 26 If Satan cast out Satan, he is divided against himself. how then will his kingdom stand? 27 And if I cast out demons by Beelzebub, by whom do your sons cast them out? therefore they shall be your judges. 28 But if I cast out demons by the Spirit of God, surely the kingdom of God has come upon you."* **Matthew 12:22-28**

The Anointing

In verse twenty eight Jesus says, *"...if I cast out demons by the Spirit of God, surely the kingdom of God has come upon you..."*. In a parallel, or at least very similar account to this same incident recorded by Luke, Jesus used different terminology to describe the ability by which He cast out demons.

> *"14 And He was casting out a demon, and it was mute. So it was, when the demon had gone out, that the mute spoke; and the multitudes marveled. 15 But some of them said, "He casts out demons by Beelzebub, the ruler of the demons." 16 Others, testing Him, sought from Him a sign from heaven. 17 But He, knowing their thoughts, said to them: "Every kingdom divided against itself is brought to desolation, and a house divided against a house falls. 18 If Satan also is divided against himself, how will his kingdom stand? Because you say I cast out demons by Beelzebub. 19 And if I cast out demons by Beelzebub, by whom do your sons cast them out? Therefore they will be your judges. 20 But if I cast out demons with the finger of God, surely the kingdom of God has come upon you."*
> **Luke 11:14-20**

In verse twenty Jesus says, *"...if I cast out demons with the finger of God, surely the kingdom of God has come upon you..."*. *"The Spirit of God..."* and *"...the finger of God..."* are not two different sources of ability by which Jesus cast out demons. They are simply two different names by which one source of ability is referred.

We have already seen with simplicity and clarity how Jesus used different names to refer to the Spirit of God to help us better understand how to relate to the Holy Spirit. Diversity of names is a common practice in God. Isaiah prophesied of Jesus using a diversity of names.

*"6 For unto us a Child is born, unto us a Son is given; and the government will be upon His shoulder. **And His name will be called Wonderful, Counselor, Mighty God, Everlasting Father, Prince of Peace." Isaiah 9:6***

Jesus broke the yoke of demonic bondage from the lives of everyone out of whom He cast demons. The ability by which He fulfilled this aspect of His ministry was the Spirit of God, also called the Finger of God. Isaiah wrote of the yoke of bondage being broken by yet another name.

*"27 The yoke will be destroyed because of the anointing." **Isaiah 10:27 KJV***

Jesus destroyed the yoke of demonic bondage because of the Anointing, also called the Spirit of God and the Finger of God. This is only one aspect of His ministry being fulfilled in the ability of the Holy Spirit, the Anointing of God. Let us refer back to **Luke 4:18,19** to consider other aspects of Jesus' ministry.

*"18 The Spirit of the Lord is upon Me, because He has anointed Me to preach the gospel to the poor; He has sent Me to heal the brokenhearted, to proclaim liberty to the captives and recovery of sight to the blind, to set at liberty those who are oppressed; 19 To proclaim the acceptable year of the Lord." **Luke 4:18.19***

Preaching, teaching, healing, and deliverance are all included in the prophetic fulfillment of the Word of God spoken through Isaiah. Jesus preached in the Anointing, taught in the Anointing, healed in the Anointing, and cast out demons in the Anointing. In other words, Jesus preached, taught, healed, and cast out demons in the ability, provision, capacity, or qualification with which the Spirit of God provided.

Now we can add to our statement of purpose for the Anointing, the special endowment (ability, provision, capacity, or qualification) of the Spirit of God. The top priority of the Spirit of God as the Anointing to believers is still to provide us with the ability to know Jesus and the Father. What we add to our top priority statement will be very simple. It comes out of knowing God. The Spirit of God as the Anointing is to provide us with the ability to carry out great exploits as the Father wills. Daniel spoke by inspiration of the Spirit of God in this same matter.

> *"32 The people who know their God shall be strong, and carry out great exploits."* **Daniel 11:32**

This will include preaching, teaching, healing, casting out demons, and all else the Father wills for us to do. Let us write the purpose of the Anointing in easy to read form. The purpose of the Anointing in the lives of believers is to provide us with the ability, provision, capacity, or qualification to:

1. Know God, and out of that knowledege to...

2. Carry out great exploits as the Father wills!

ANOINTED TO DO EXPLOITS

We will begin to consider what exploits the Father wills for us with the words Jesus spoke to His disciples at the last supper. He said,

> *"12 Most assuredly, I say to you, he who believes in Me, the works that I do he will do also; and greater works than these he will do, because I go to My Father. 13 And whatever you ask in My name, that I will do, that the Father may be glorified in the Son. 14 If you ask anything in My name, I will do it."* ***John 14:12-14***

Jesus is speaking very plainly here. He says, *"...he who believes in Me, the works that I do he will do also..."*. Every believer is expected to do the same works, great exploits, Jesus did. Beginning with overcoming sin in our lives, to preaching the good news, laying on of hands, or casting out demons, we are to do the works of Jesus. This is the Father's will. Just as for Jesus, the Spirit of the Lord as the Anointing will cause us to be able to fulfill the Father's will as we live on the earth.

Other exploits the Father wills for us will be determined by our individual callings within the Body of Christ. Paul wrote, *"There are differences of ministries, but the same Lord"*. In his letter to the church at Ephesus he identified some of the differences of ministries.

> *"1 I, therefore, the prisoner of the Lord, beseech you to walk worthy of the calling with which you were called. 2 with all lowliness and gentleness, with longsuffering, bearing with one another in love, 3 endeavoring to keep*

the unity of the Spirit, just as you were called in one hope of your calling; 5 one Lord, one faith, one baptism; 6 one God and Father of all, who is above all, and through all, and in you all. 7 But to each one of us grace was given according to the measure of Christ's gift. 8 Therefore He says: When He ascended on high, He led captivity captive, and gave gifts to men. 9 (Now this, He ascended what does it mean but that He also first descended into the lower parts of the earth? 10 He who descended is also the One who ascended far above all the heavens, that He might fill all things.) 11 And He Himself gave some to be apostles, some prophets, some evangelists, and some pastors and teachers." **Ephesians 4:1-11**

Paul was called to be an apostle. The anointing (ability, provision, capacity, or qualification) Paul needed to fulfill his apostolic ministry was unique to the office of apostle. Agabus was called to be a prophet. The anointing Agabus needed to fulfill his prophetic ministry was unique to the office of prophet. It was the same Spirit of God who dwelt in both men. However, the Spirit of God as the Anointing provided each man with a different ability, provision, capacity or qualification (anointing) to fulfill his individual ministry.

The Spirit of God and the Anointing are two different names for the same member of the Godhead. There is only one Spirit of God as the Anointing, but He manifests Himself and His ability differently in different situations in order to help us do the will of God.

"1 Now concerning spiritual gifts, brethren, I do not want you to be ignorant: 2 You know that you were Gentiles, carried away to these dumb idols, however you were led. 3 Therefore I make known to you that no one speaking by the Spirit of God calls Jesus accursed, and no one can say that Jesus is Lord except by the Holy

Spirit. 4 There are diversities of gifts, but the same Spirit. 5 There are differences of ministries, but the same Lord. 6 And there are diversities of activities, but it is the same God who works all in all." **I Corinthians 12:1-6**

The Spirit of God as the Anointing who abides within you will manifest Himself and His ability according to your calling or need to help you do the will of God. The Spirit of God as the Anointing will provide you with His ability to pastor if you are called to be a pastor. The Spirit of God as the Anointing will provide you with His ability to evangelize if you are called to be a evangelist. The Spirit of God as the Anointing will provide you with whatever ability you need to do whatever God has willed you to do.

If you need to cast out a demon, the Spirit of God as the Anointing will provide you with the anointing (ability) to cast the demon out. If you need to lay hands on someone for them to be healed, the Spirit of God as the Anointing will provide you with the ability (anointing) to lay on hands so the person may recover.

FLOWING IN THE ANOINTING

Many believers have been led astray searching for another man's anointing. It is a common belief among many the anointing can be transferred from one to another. In one sense the anointing can be transferred by the laying on of hands if you mean a person can receive the Holy Spirit who is the Anointing as a gift from the Father when hands are laid on him.

However, it is not possible for a gift of ministry to lay hands on a person who is not called to an office of ministry and transfer ministry gift anointing into the person. The Spirit of God as the Anointing works in agreement with the will of the Father. If the Father did not call you to an office of ministry, no man can transfer anointing into you to make you fulfill the work of an office of ministry.

A person, who is called to an office of ministry and flows in the anointing of his office, can help another person called to an office of ministry learn how to flow in the anointing. The anointing is simply the ability, provision, capacity, or qualification provided by the Spirit of God as the Anointing. The anointing (ability, provision, capacity, or qualification) for one office of ministry is different from the anointing of another office of ministry. However, the Spirit of God as the Anointing is the same in the lives of both persons standing in different offices of ministry.

There is only one Spirit of God as the Anointing. The Spirit of God and the Anointing are one in the same. There is only one Anointing. The Spirit of God as the Anointing will manifest Himself in a diversity of ways but He remains the same Holy Spirit, Anointing.

The number one priority for the believer is to grow in knowledge and understanding of who the Holy Spirit is and how to flow together with Him to know God. Remember the top priority of the Spirit of God as the Anointing is to provide us with the ability to know Jesus and the Father. As the believer becomes accustomed to receiving the anointing to know God, it will be easier to receive the anointing to minister to others. The same Holy Spirit as the Anointing manifests Himself in a diversity of ways. One way provides you with the ability to know God; another way provides you with the ability to minister to others.

Chapter Nine

SUMMARY AND CONCLUSION

Perhaps the most vital revelation contained within this book is the emphasis on developing relationship with God! The Triune God has not given us *"...the spirit of bondage again to fear, but you received the Spirit of adoption by whom we cry out, Abba, Father. The Spirit Himself bears witness with our spirit that we are children of God..."* **Romans 8:15,16**. Because our heavenly Father has placed such a premium on relationship, His provision for us to obtain eternal life is to know Him and Jesus.

> *"3 This is eternal life, that they may know You, the only true God, and Jesus Christ whom You have sent!"* **John 17:3**

Once we understand the Father's desire for us to know the Trinity and to fellowship together it will change our perspective of God, of Christianity, and of ministry.

Too often service is emphasized even above knowing God. When that happens, service becomes bondage and servitude. God does want us to serve Him but from a relationship of sonship not servitude. I remember in my own life and ministry how lack of proper understanding took me in the wrong direction. Service had been the predominant theme in almost every Christian circle in which I had been a part. I believed the more I could serve God with my life and ministry, the more I would please God.

Once during a ministry trip to Lansing, Michigan I was fasting and praying for our daily meetings. While lying on the bed in my motel room, I was seeking God as to how I could serve Him more efficiently. How I could go to more places in the world to minister to more people.

Suddenly the Spirit of the Lord spoke to me on behalf of the Father. He said, *"Son you are more important to me than your ministry! I did not redeem you to be My servant. I redeemed you to be My son"*. These words pinned me to the bed, frozen in thought for what seemed like an eternity.

Finally, I began to test the spirit to see if He really was the Spirit of the Lord. He does not mind being tested if we want to know the Truth. I said, "That challenges what I have believed all my life. If that is really you, Holy Spirit, please show me in scripture what you spoke to me". He took me to three places in scripture. The first place He took me was in the first letter Paul wrote to the church at Corinth.

> *"19 Do you not know that your body is the temple of the Holy Spirit who is in you, whom you have from God, and you are not your own? 20 For you were bought at a price; therefore glorify God in your body and in your spirit, which are God's."* **I Corinthians 6:19,10**

I responded, "That seems to support what I have always believed. I belong to God, purchased with a price to be His servant".

The Holy Spirit took me to the second place in scripture:

"18 You were not redeemed with corruptible things, like silver or gold, from your aimless conduct received by tradition from your fathers, 19 but with the precious blood of Christ, as of a lamb without blemish and without spot. 20 He indeed was foreordained before the foundation of the world, but was manifest in these last times for you 21 who through Him believe in God, who raised Him from the dead and gave Him glory, so that your faith and hope are in God." **I Peter 1:18-21**

He then said, *"In many parts of the world today you can still purchase servants if you have the money to do so. The Father owns the cattle on a thousand hills and the earth and the fullness thereof are His. If He was only interested in purchasing servants to do His work, would He have paid such a dear price for your redemption?"*

Then, He took me to the third place in scripture:

"1 Now I say that the heir, as long as he is a child, does not differ at all from a slave, though he is master of all, 2 but is under guardians and stewards until the time appointed by the father. 3 Even so we, when we were children, were in bondage under the elements of the world. 4 But when the fullness of the time had come, God sent forth His Son, born of a woman, born under the law, 5 to redeem those who were under the law, that we might receive the adoption as sons. 6 And because you are sons, God has sent forth the Spirit of His Son into your hearts, crying out, Abba Father! 7 Therefore you are no longer a slave but a son, and if a son, then an heir of God through Christ." **Galatians 4:1-7**

I could see very clearly what the Holy Spirit was showing me, but the tradition and doctrine of man was so deeply ingrained within me that it was difficult to let them go.

I thought out loud, "Then are we not to serve? Am I not to be a servant of the Lord? And if we do not serve, then how will the work of God be done in the earth?"

The Holy Spirit corrected my wrong thinking. He said, *"I did not say you were not to serve. I said you were not redeemed to be a servant. You were redeemed to be a son. As you are established in your relationship with the Father as His son, you will serve out of love and desire not out of bondage and servitude."*

He showed me Jesus as illustration of what He was teaching me. If there was ever a person on earth who had a revelation of God as Father and Himself as Son, it was Jesus. Even at twelve years old returning from Jerusalem to Nazareth when Jesus stayed behind in the Temple, He understood Father-Son relationship.

> *"48 So when they saw Him, they were amazed; and His mother said to Him, "Son, why have You done this to us? Look, Your father and I have sought You anxiously." 49 And He said to them, "Why did you seek Me? Did you not know that I must be about My Father's business?" 50 But they did not understand the statement which He spoke to them."* **Luke 2:48-50**

Jesus understood that God was His Father, but He also served the Father. He served His Father as a Son not as a servant. Jesus understood the difference perfectly. He told His disciples,

> *"15 No longer do I call you servants, for a servant does not know what his master is doing; but I have called you friends, for all things that I heard from My Father I have made known to you."* **John 15:15**

Summary

Jesus knew what His Father was doing. In fact He said,

> *"Most assuredly, I say to you, the Son can do nothing of Himself, but what He sees the Father do; for whatever He does, the Son also does in like manner. For the Father loves the Son and shows Him all things that He Himself does; and He will show Him greater works than these, that you may marvel."* **John 5:19,20**

Jesus understood His sonship yet served the Father. He served the Father because He loved the Father and was in agreement with the Father's plan for salvation. ***Service from any other perspective in the New Covenant is not according to the will of God.***

Consider the older brother in the account of the prodigal son. Generally we hear the parable taught from the perspective of the younger son. However, there is also a profound truth to be learned from the older son. We know the younger son received his inheritance early, left home, and squandered his money on riotous living. From the fields with the swine the young man came to his senses and returned home. His father received him again saying, *"...this my son was dead and is alive again; he was lost and is found." And they began to be merry"* ***Luke 15:24.***

> *"25 Now his older son was in the field. And as he came and drew near to the house, he heard music and dancing. 26 So he called one of the servants and asked what these things meant. 27 And he said to him, 'Your brother has come, and because he has received him safe and sound, your father has killed the fatted calf.' 28 But he was angry and would not go in. Therefore his father came out and pleaded with him. 29 So he answered and said*

177

to his father, 'Lo, these many years I have been serving you; I never transgressed your commandment at any time; and yet you never gave me a young goat, that I might make merry with my friends. 30 But as soon as this son of yours came, who has devoured your livelihood with harlots, you killed the fatted calf for him.' 31 And he said to him, 'Son, you are always with me, and all that I have is yours. 32 It was right that we should make merry and be glad, for your brother was dead and is alive again, and was lost and is found." **Luke 15:25-32**

Two very profound statements, one made by each the older son and the father, are found in this portion of scripture. Notice the older son's statement first from verse twenty-nine. ***"Lo, these many years I have been serving you; I never transgressed your commandment at any time; and yet you never gave me a young goat, that I might make merry with my friends."*** The older son had a heart to serve, but it was the heart of a servant not the heart of a son. He served and obeyed in every detail but was full of frustration, anger, and bitterness because he had not received the reward he felt he justly deserved. This son did not have an understanding of sonship.

The father's reply from verse thirty-one confirms the older son's lack of understanding. ***"Son, you are always with me, and all that I have is yours."*** The very first word out of the father's mouth correctly identifies the proper role for the young man, ***"...son..."***! Secondly, the father correctly identifies the proper relationship between a son and his father, ***"...you are always with me, and all that I have is yours".***

178

Summary

Service in the kingdom of God without understanding sonship will typically cause us to miss our Father-son relationship and the benefits that go with it. However, service from a proper role of son to Father will promote a healthy relationship including the benefits that go with it. Once we understand the Father's desire for us to know the Trinity and to serve from the perspective of sons, our lives and ministries will surely change!

This book is about knowing God! It is about God the Holy Spirit whose primary responsibility is to help us know our God. The Father has assigned the responsibility to *"...guide us into all truth..."* to the *"...Spirit of truth..."*. However, we have seen the Father's will does not operate automatically, it must be activated by faith. We have learned we obtain faith in order to be able to activate the Father's will for our lives through knowledge and understanding. This book was written to help us know and understand the Father's will concerning the person and ministry of the Holy Spirit. Once we have grown in knowledge and understanding of who the Holy Spirit is, the proper basis to relate to Him, and how to receive ministry from Him, we will be better prepared in faith and ability to know God.

The revelation contained within this book is only a seed. If you are born again, then you are good soil. I pray for you that as you look to God to give the increase, you will receive a harvest of abundance!

Made in the USA
Charleston, SC
12 April 2013